Amish
by Adoption

ISBN: 978-1-941213-83-4

Cover and text layout design: Kristi Yoder

Printed in the USA
Second printing: January 2016

Published by:
TGS International
P.O. Box 355
Berlin, Ohio 44610 USA
Phone: 330.893.4828
Fax: 330.893.2305
www.tgsinternational.com

TGS001167

Amish
by Adoption

Lily A. Bear

"They that wait upon the LORD shall renew their strength; they shall mount up with wings as eagles; they shall run, and not be weary; and they shall walk, and not faint."
Isaiah 40:31

"As an eagle stirreth up her nest, fluttereth over her young, spreadeth abroad her wings, taketh them, beareth them on her wings, so the LORD alone did lead him . . ."
Deuteronomy 32:11, 12

Dedication

Dedicated to every "Andy" who has blessed a childless home with love and joy, giving parents and child the privilege of being a family.

Table of Contents

Introduction

While all children face challenges as they grow to adulthood, those who are adopted face some challenges not faced by those who are raised by their biological parents. Most adopted children have been rejected either at birth or later in life. This rejection is real and often affects their physical, emotional, and intellectual growth and behavior. In addition, adopted children inherit personality traits from their biological parents that may differ from those of their adopted families.

Each adopted child copes differently but most of them live with unanswered questions such as: Who am I? Why didn't my mother want me? Do I look like her? What about my father? Do I have siblings?

Andy King is an adopted child. I met him years after his adoption on a picturesque Amish farm where he lives with his wife Sarah and their ten children. The family impressed me as being friendly, hardworking, and peaceful. I was challenged as I observed the parents' diligence in daily prayer and Bible reading as they taught their children about God.

As Andy thinks about his adoption, he does not ask, *Why me?* Instead he shares this testimony:

"Personally, I am thankful I was adopted. I have truly been blessed to be raised in a Christian home. I hope I can, with God's help, live a life that shows my appreciation."

Though Andy has struggled with the questions that adopted children must face, he has come to accept this as God's plan for his life. Because of this acceptance, God is using him to help others with similar stories come to a place of peace.

To protect the family's privacy, names and locations have been changed throughout this book. Other details have also been added or changed in the telling of Andy's story. With Andy's consent, the symbol of the bald eagle has been woven throughout this book to demonstrate his love for nature and portray his childhood struggles and victories.

Andy's story is uniquely his. As he shares it, may your love and understanding for adopted children deepen and grow.

—Lily A. Bear

Prologue

Another horse and buggy! Where exactly are we going? Are we headed to an Amish farm? Allison Bentley grabbed the armrest as her husband Rod hit the brakes. Her stomach tightened another notch. She leaned forward, trying to see around the sharp bend and the dawdling horse and buggy taking up two-thirds of their lane on this curvy country road.

As Rod and Allison's red Oldsmobile wound its way along the unfamiliar back roads, forty-three-year-old Andy King was standing on his parents' porch talking with his mother. "My sister and her family are coming today, Mom. Sorry, I should have told you sooner."

Fanny King fingered the edge of her apron. Her pulse jumped at the thought of this meeting. "Did you tell her you're Amish?" She looked up into the face of her son, hating to ask, but wanting to know if the people who were coming knew they were meeting an Amish sibling. Ever since Andy had asked her and Mark how they felt about him searching for his biological family, she had feared that a meeting like this would bring more disappointment and rejection to their son.

Her husband Mark had had no qualms about their son

searching for his roots, but Fanny had found it hard to say, "Yes, go ahead." She had wanted to cry out, "No! Don't do it! Don't do something that might bring you more heartache."

Did their son realize the depth of their love? He was the first child they could claim as their very own. He was the son she had longed and prayed for. The son she had held and cuddled. The son who had filled the void of empty arms and a longing heart, the son she had cried over, laughed with, taught, and disciplined. This tall, gentle, fine son who had a family of his own—would he need to bear yet another rejection? Seven years of searching, and now—this meeting.

"No, Mom." Andy let out a frustrated sigh. "Sarah asked me the same thing, but each time I talked on the phone with my sister, the timing never seemed right." Inside, Andy thought, *How could I blurt out, "Hey! I'm Amish!" If I had told her, she might have refused to meet me, and I do want to see and talk to my own blood relative at least this one time.* He saw a red car slow down, round the bend in the road at the end of their lane, and stop. He heard the gears shifting and saw the car begin to climb their long, sloping driveway.

"She's here!" he whispered. Fanny saw her son's left eye twitch, the same nervous reaction that had plagued him as a boy when experiencing bouts of rejection, insecurity, or trauma.

"Dear God, for his sake, let this meeting go well," her mother heart pleaded as she watched her son walk across the lawn toward his own house and the arriving car.

". . . and I brought photos of our mom." The words of the dark-haired woman he had just met, his newfound sister, pulled at him like a magnet. His hand trembled as he took the photo, and for the first time in his forty-three years he saw the face of the mother who had given him birth.

Jan

1

1965

J an O'Connor peeked out from behind the living room drapes at the two army boys talking to her older brothers. The one with reddish hair was certainly good-looking. If she could get him to pay attention to her this weekend, her boyfriend Kurt would be furious. Wouldn't that be fun! Her cheeks flushed at the challenge, and she tossed her head, shaking her dark curls until they fanned in a riot around her face. Her friends said she was cute. She loved the admiration she received from her stunning head of hair. So what if Kurt got mad! He needn't think he owned her.

Though Jan would not be a teen until October, her height, build, and manner made her appear older. Being left to fend for herself while her mom worked late hours at the local bar, with her father stationed elsewhere with the military, and her older brothers busy with their lives, made Jan streetwise and responsible to no one. It was intoxicating when her brothers' friends made a pass at her, and her brothers didn't mind having a kid sister around that their friends liked.

Jan tossed her head again, ready for the challenge of these strangers in army uniforms and crew cuts. Smoothing her wrinkled blouse, she grabbed a cold Coke from the refrigerator, squared her shoulders, and sauntered casually out the door with her face turned in the opposite direction of the boys. A whistle shattered the normal street noise, and Jan stopped in her tracks. Feigning surprise, she swung around to face the boys, her eyes wide in question as if she had no prior knowledge of their presence.

"She your cute kid sister?" the good-looking boy asked. Jan flashed him a dazzling smile. "Thanks!" she said, "But don't ask my brothers. They would never admit it!"

"Name's Bob," he introduced himself. "I'm visiting some friends while on break from spring training. You are definitely cute!" His voice dropped as he asked, "See you around?" His half question sent tingles through her and, giving him a shy smile, she turned around and re-entered the house, hoping he would soon follow.

Bob didn't waste time in showing her he liked being with her. During the next week he almost lived at their place, and Jan fell completely under his spell. She welcomed his attention until she lost herself, mind, soul, and body, believing this was love that would never end.

Bob returned to army training while Jan lived in a dream, the envy of her sixth-grade classmates. To have an eighteen-year-old falling head-over-heels for you! Her friends were envious. They fought to be with her, yet hated the attention she received. Jan was in her element. So what if she had to repeat sixth grade! Knowing Bob gave her the edge. That placed her in a bracket above all her classmates.

A week before school dismissed for the summer, Jan's mother returned home from work to find her daughter vomiting in the bathroom.

"What's going on?" she demanded.

"I don't know," Jan wailed. "It's been hitting me off and on all week!"

Deeper probing soon had her mother furious. "I've told you to stay away from boys! All they are is trouble!" she yelled.

"Where were your brothers when Bob was here? Why didn't they look out for you! Some family I raised! I break my back working to keep you kids decent, and you turn around and shame me like this? If I could just get my hands on that no-account Bob . . ." she spat out the words.

"Mom," Jan sobbed, "I am only sick, and you scream at me. I can't help it!"

"No, I guess you can't." In a rare show of emotion, Marsha O'Connor gathered her daughter into her arms as she cried, "Jan, Jan, my baby, oh, this is a cruel world. What are we going to do?"

That evening Jan's whole world came crashing down around her. Before the month was up, her safe, carefree world of friends, school, and small-town activities became distant memories. Jan O'Connor discovered she would become a mother two months after her thirteenth birthday.

Jan found herself uprooted from everything familiar when her mother placed her under the temporary care of the Child Welfare Board, who sent her to a city home for unwed mothers. There was nothing glamorous about her restricted life now. She hated Bob for making her leave her family but longed for him to show up at the home and make things right.

Unknown to Jan's family, the welfare board had reported

Bob's felony. When Bob realized he was to be court-martialed, he took his own life with his army rifle. It would be many years before any of Jan's family learned of his death.

Baby Boy O'Connor

2

December 1965-July 1966

Newborn Baby Boy O'Connor took his first struggling breath in Grants Hospital. His weak cry gave hope to the delivery doctor that this little five-pound-two-and-a-half-ounce miracle just might have a fighting chance to survive.

"It is only two days before Christmas, and you are all alone in this world, you dear, sweet bit of heaven," the motherly nurse in charge murmured as she wrapped his cool body in a blanket and placed him in the incubator. Jan's twenty-one hours of labor had prepared the entire floor for the coming of this event. "Poor little-girl mother," the nurse murmured as she cast a pitying glance at the sleeping form. The ordeal had been long and hard, but Jan would never reap the joys of her travail or even hold this precious bundle. The entire staff was aware of the signed papers at the nurses' station, papers belonging to Social Services, bearing Jan's signature and signing all rights for her baby's care over to them. At birth, newborn O'Connor had become the state's responsibility.

"Poor dear baby, I pray God will give you a good home and a good life." The nurse patted him gently, letting him know she cared. "Poor baby, I wonder what will happen to you."

When Jan was released from the hospital, she walked out as a young girl, supposedly freed from the stigma of having had an illegitimate child. Though she was told she had no responsibility concerning her child, the Social Service workers never told Jan she would leave a part of herself behind in the life of her unseen, unnamed baby.

For Jan's mother Marsha, it wasn't until Jan returned home alone that reality sank in. *Jan's baby would be my grandson! What was I thinking? Why did I let the welfare board have full responsibility for this child?* She felt like tearing her hair out as she sat alone at the empty table while sleep claimed the rest of her family.

"Everything falls on me," she moaned bitterly. "Everything!" Her thoughts ran on. *Husband always gone and kids running wild! Bills and more bills. What else was I to do but let them take care of everything? But how cruel is this? Not even a chance to see my own grandson!*

"Well, I will just change that!" Marsha rose from the table, fiercely determined to make this wrong right, no matter what other people would say when she brought the baby home.

"Jan, I'm buying a bassinet and bringing your baby home to raise," she informed her startled daughter the next morning.

"I never even got to see my baby," Jan murmured as she stared off into nothing. "They told me I was too young to be a mother. They said it was best to forget about my baby and just go back to school and be with my friends again. They said I had a whole life ahead of me to live. Who do you think my baby looks like? What if he has curly hair like mine? That would be cute, wouldn't it?" she asked her mother.

Marsha glanced sharply at her daughter. *Why hadn't they let her hold her baby? Was he okay? Was there a chance he had some type of deformity?* A great longing seized her. Marsha was baffled by these feelings of protective tenderness that eroded the tough exterior of her life. She only knew she wanted to hold this newborn grandson, to watch him breathe, to feel the softness of his skin, to see if he did look like her daughter. She wanted to know all about this little baby her daughter knew nothing about.

"I'll get him. I'll bring him home as soon as I can get away," she promised Jan. "After all, I am the grandmother. We should have no problem getting him back."

Several days passed before Marsha could work on fulfilling her promise. *This will be kind of fun,* she thought as she entered the hospital. *Besides, Jan needs more responsibility when I'm working at night. Taking care of a baby would surely keep her at home more.*

"Where is my daughter's baby?" Marsha asked for the third time, frustrated because no one at the hospital would give her any information. Baby Boy O'Connor seemed to have evaporated into thin air.

"I'm making some phone calls. Give me a few minutes," the receptionist assured her as she rose and entered a closed door behind her.

"I'm sorry, Mrs. O'Connor," she informed the waiting woman when she returned. "You will have to talk to the Child Welfare Board. I understand your daughter was a dependent with them before she had her baby. Release papers were signed before the birth, and there is nothing the hospital can do to help you. All information will have to come from the County Welfare Board."

"Can I talk to them by telephone?" Marsha asked. "I need to be home this afternoon in time to go to work."

"I'll dial the number for you," the receptionist said as she graciously did so, handing over the receiver.

"They never expected the baby to live?" The receptionist doodled with her pen but listened closely to each word Marsha repeated.

She watched as Mrs. O'Connor's shoulders sagged, and felt a twinge of pity for her. "Then you can't help me," she heard Marsha speak into the receiver as she ended the phone call.

Marsha looked at the receptionist hopelessly as she handed her the receiver. "They said my grandson never had a chance to live. They had no hope that he would survive. He had physical complications. Was not strong enough. Nothing's fair in this world!" Her clipped, bitter tone startled the receptionist, who made no reply. She watched as Marsha exited the hospital, glad there had been no further confrontation.

I'll have to believe it, even if I don't want to. It's true. Jan's baby was born and died without even a grandmother to shed a tear over him. A sharp pain stabbed her; she would never see or hold her tiny grandson. Jan would never get to mother her baby.

Marsha, however, did not know the whole truth. She did not know that Baby Boy O'Connor had been placed in a foster home six days after birth and was still very much alive.

Two days after Baby Boy O'Connor arrived in her home, Mrs. Craig, his concerned foster mother, took the baby to the hospital.

"This baby is not well. Look at his motley skin! And he barely sucks! I'm terribly worried," Mrs. Craig told Dr. Morrison before he started his examination.

"Yes, we have a very sick baby here. Let me call Grants Hospital and get information on his release."

The doctor soon returned and shared the results of his telephone conversation with Mrs. Craig. "Grants Hospital discharged this baby with no problems except that of being a reluctant eater. I don't have all the information, but I'm guessing the child was a preemie and was discharged too early. Now, he's going to have to improve quickly if he is going to live. If you know how to pray, do so."

Days passed, and Baby O'Connor remained in serious condition. One day during a bout of retching, he aspirated seriously, drawing liquid into his lungs. He stopped breathing but soon revived. But then he developed pneumonia. Miraculously, he recovered.

Baby O'Connor was bathed, fed, and changed when needed. He was physically well cared for, but no mother lavished on him a mother's love. He did not grow well. Four weeks after his birth, on January 21, his weight was recorded as "5 pounds 12 ounces." Baby O'Connor had gained only six ounces since birth.

Dr. Morrison put the baby on a soybean formula to see if he would gain weight. "Keep this baby in an upright position for one to one-and-a half hours after each feeding," he instructed the nurses. Within five days of the nurses following these instructions, Baby O'Connor had gained a whopping three-fourth pound! Dr. Morrison was happy with the gain and sent him home to Mrs. Craig with strict instructions to continue the sitting position after each feeding.

Mrs. Craig began calling the nameless baby "Connor." At his next two-week checkup, Connor had gained another nine ounces, but his weak cry and listlessness showed something was seriously wrong. "Do you think he can see?" Mrs. Craig asked. "He certainly doesn't act like a normal baby."

"I tend to agree with you," Dr. Morrison acknowledged. "It is likely he also has some central nervous system insult that has been responsible for his poor feeding history. This may have been further aggravated by the distress suffered by the aspiration incident."

"What do you mean?" Mrs. Craig questioned.

"To translate it simply, Baby Connor may have cerebral palsy."

"Poor baby," Mrs. Craig murmured in a rare show of pity as she tucked his blanket firmly around him. "Who will want this baby now?" she asked.

Dr. Morrison sent the following report to the Custody of Child Welfare Board:

Baby Boy O'Connor was examined by ophthalmologist Dr. Letson on March 11, 1966. On examination he found the optic nerve pale. Dr. Letson felt there might be damage to the central nervous system and that the baby is practically blind.

March 19 found Connor back in the hospital for another few days. On his chart was written: "Listlessness and poor eating. Found low blood count. Medication given."

In April, when Connor's caseworker, Mrs. Sims, paid a visit at the Craig home she called attention to the appearance of his head. "Notice how his right side is larger than his left side."

"It is, isn't it? Maybe that is why he always turns his head to the right side no matter how I place him. Something is definitely wrong," Mrs. Craig agreed.

By the end of April, Connor's general appearance had improved, and Dr. Morrison was pleased. He asked Dr. Letson to examine him again as there was still a question about possible cerebral palsy. It was not until the end of June that Dr. Letson examined him. He, too, was pleased with Connor's progress, but he gave a guarded evaluation of his degree of sight, and he felt that the boy still showed signs of cerebral palsy.

On July 13, 1966, a developmental evaluation was done to determine Connor's intellectual potential and neurological status. Baby O'Connor's health had improved enough for him to be considered ready for adoption placement. His medical records stated that he would be placed "as a handicapped child due to abnormal neurological signs of a marked degree which would warrant a diagnosis of cerebral palsy in an older child."

Mark and Fanny King

3

Fall 1966

"That wraps up my work here," Fanny King announced to her empty house as she wiped out her cleaning bucket that fall afternoon. All their furniture and extra belongings had been put in storage in preparation for the new renters moving in at the beginning of November. "I do hope I packed everything we'll need for the next two years!" Mentally she checked off her list. Sewing machine, dishes, clothes, canned goods, dry staples she had on hand, the Bible, Mark's study books . . . "Doesn't seem like much," she mused. Two whole years! It seemed like a lifetime stretching endlessly before her. Two years without their family or friends or church.

If only we were blessed with children, Mark would be exempt from doing I-W service. The familiar thoughts trailed through Fanny's mind again. Her husband Mark was registered with the government as a conscientious objector to war. Because he had no children, and because he was under twenty-six years of age, Mark was required by law to do two years of alternative service. Fanny's deep sigh echoed through the stillness of the kitchen where she lingered. It spilled out into the living area, growing more potent until its longing threatened to suffocate the young wife.

A tear escaped. Another followed suit. "It's not fair!" she sobbed. "We just celebrated our fourth wedding anniversary, and we still don't have children! It's over two years since we applied for adoption, and nothing! Not once has the agency written!" As she brushed away her tears, she wished that was all it took to wipe away her heartache.

"Forget the tears! Weeping has never helped. You must act like a responsible married woman instead of the young and flighty Fanny Yoder!" she scolded herself grimly.

"Mark says God will provide in His time. For now, he tells me God needs us to serve faithfully in the hospital." A half sob, half laugh, replaced her sadness when she recalled the look on her husband's face as he had read what his job would be at the hospital.

"Washing dishes!" he had sputtered. "It says here I am to report to the hospital kitchen October 18 to fulfill dishwashing responsibilities. Fanny, do they expect me to wash all the dishes used in the hospital?" His look of horror had been priceless. Full-blown laughter rippled through the empty house at the memory.

She sobered. She believed that Mark was right and that someday God would give them children. But the waiting was not easy. Whenever friends held newborn babies or their conversations centered on babies and active toddlers, she felt she had nothing to contribute. What did she know of sleepless nights, teething, sick babies, housework that piled up, or sheer exhaustion? The longer she and Mark remained childless, she seemed to find less and less common ground with other wives.

Maybe I am glad Mark has to do two years of service. At

least we will be in a different setting! She tried to be positive about the change in their lives, but what would she do with all the empty time when Mark was at work? How would she stay sane when their living quarters would consist of just a tiny one-bedroom apartment? She dreaded living among strangers, but Mark would need to do his 1-W service at a hospital two hours from their home community.

Later that afternoon, Fanny entered her in-laws' home to find a letter waiting for her and Mark. She glanced at the return address to see who had sent it. Her heart began beating rapidly when she saw the words: Child Welfare Board.

Ripping open the envelope, Fanny read in breathless wonder:

> Dear Mr. and Mrs. King,
>
> I am writing to inquire if you are still interested in adopting a child. We have a 9½-month-old handicapped baby. Call me if you are interested. Telephone extension: 2-2292
>
> Lorena Sims
> Executive Secretary
> Child Welfare Board

"Mom! There is a baby for us! And Mark has to start work in the hospital on Monday. What are we to do?" *A baby!* Fanny felt like dancing in circles. So what if the baby was handicapped! She and Mark would love the baby anyway. "Oh, Mom, do you think Mark will get an exemption?"

"Calm down, Fanny." Her mother-in-law shook her finger playfully at her. She didn't blame Fanny for her excitement though. Her own joy overflowed as she thanked God for intervening and answering her prayer. Ever since Mark had been called to serve his 1-W time at the distant hospital, she had felt burdened. Being tied to the city for two years without a church or church family was bound to affect Mark and Fanny's spiritual health. Would they be able to keep the faith while living for two years in a secular environment? The only thing she had known to do was to pray that God would keep Mark and Fanny from going. There was no question in her mind now that this was God's answer to her prayer.

After supper Mark took the letter and went to talk to Atlee Miller, a Mennonite neighbor man who helped the area's conscientious objectors find places to do their 1-W service.

"This changes the picture completely," Atlee said after reading the letter. "Since you had applied for adoption over two years ago, I don't see any reason why you will not be exempted. Taking a handicapped child may also be in your favor.

"I would go ahead and set up an appointment with the adoption agency. Tomorrow I will contact our district's office and let them know what is happening. If you don't hear from me tomorrow, you will know you are approved for exemption.

"And congratulations! Best wishes as you become parents."

Things moved quickly after the phone call to Mrs. Lorena Sims. Mrs. Sims accepted Fanny's invitation for lunch the following Tuesday. Furniture had to be brought out of storage and the renters notified of their change of plans. By Tuesday, Fanny had her house in order and a delicious fried chicken dinner ready to serve. Crusty dinner rolls, mashed potatoes, dressing and gravy, fall parsnips, two kinds of home-canned pickles, and canned peaches completed her menu.

Fanny could not relax. She felt as excited as a young schoolgirl, but when Mrs. Sims arrived, she calmly dished up her dinner and acted like a responsible young wife.

Seated at the table, Mrs. Sims told Mark and Fanny that the doctor had given a guarded report of the baby's vision. He had also said that there were indications of cerebral palsy that could become more apparent and increase in severity as the baby grew older.

"If God gives us a special needs child, we will love and care for that child the best we know how," Mark assured Mrs. Sims.

"Yes, indeed," agreed Fanny. "But can you explain what the doctor meant by 'guarded'?" she asked.

"Because of the baby's age, the doctor is unable to tell how well he can see. The March examination showed that the baby was practically blind, and the June examination showed no change. But by July, the doctor felt the baby's overall health had improved enough that he could be released for adoption as a handicapped child."

"Handicapped children need love too," Fanny said softly as she swallowed the lump in her throat. "Maybe even more."

Mrs. Sims smiled at the young couple. "I knew you would take this child and love and care for him. I knew your answer when I sent the letter, but I am required to make sure you know the aspects involved in taking these children. Congratulations on your little son!"

Fanny's eyes glistened with tears of happiness. God was giving them a little son! "How soon?" she whispered, finding it hard to speak above the emotions churning within.

"Baby Connor, as his foster mother named him, is in a home an hour from here. I plan to bring him to my office tomorrow. Does it suit you to be at my office at 11:00 in the morning?"

"Yes!" Mark and Fanny answered in unison.

"I see no problem then." The caseworker loved the anticipation of these new parents. "I'm confident he will be in good hands. It is a pleasure to place a child into a home like yours. You never know what love will do for a child. Now I want to give you more information concerning your baby.

"As I said in my letter, Baby Connor is 9½ months old. He has had a rough start, and it is a miracle he is even here. Now, to help you understand how abandonment at birth affects a newborn, I will give you the following information compiled from an extensive study.

"When a baby is born, the first thing he encounters is highly traumatic fear of abandonment at being separated from his natural protector, the mother.

"A newborn baby knows his mother.

"A newborn baby is completely in tune with his mother, and why wouldn't he be? He has lived inside her all his life.

"Studies show that at birth the baby instinctively knows what his mother smells like and sounds like. He also knows how her milk tastes. Isn't that amazing?"

Mark nodded in agreement, fascinated by what he was learning. "David does say in the Psalms that we are 'fearfully and wonderfully made.' "

"How true," agreed Mrs. Sims.

"Mothers who raise their children give them stability through emotional connection," she continued. "Baby Connor has never been given that stability or connection. I am sharing this so you will understand the impact a mother's love and care has on a newborn's wellbeing.

"In the womb a baby feels warmth and security. One minute he is experiencing this safety, and the next minute, at birth, he is cold and alone, experiencing bright lights and hearing strange noises for the first time. All the newborn baby wants is comfort from his mother—her familiar voice, scent, and touch—and when the mother cuddles and nurses her child, she provides him with that security. But when a baby is taken immediately and has no contact with his mother, what does that baby suffer? What must it be like to never return to the familiar sound, scent, taste, or touch of his mother?

"This does not mean, of course, that there is no hope for a child who has been abandoned by his mother. I am telling you though so that you can better understand what this child has experienced and so that you can help to provide the love and security he has missed."

Fanny reached for her husband's hand. She needed someone to share the pain she felt as she thought of the trauma their soon-to-be son had been suffering. Mark squeezed her fingers, letting her know he felt the same, and understood.

Mrs. Sims put her papers away and stood to leave. "I will

see you tomorrow morning at 11:00," she concluded. "I am looking forward to your meeting with the baby."

Fanny sang as she cleaned up her dinner table. She sang as she put her leftover food away. She was singing when she checked the oven to make sure she had removed all the baking dishes—until she saw her roaster full of untouched fried chicken. The song died on her lips. She stood with her mouth hanging open, not believing her eyes. Of all things! How could she have forgotten to serve the chicken? Suddenly she started laughing. She laughed until tears rolled down her face and her stomach hurt. She didn't stop laughing until she realized she was crying. Crying for her baby, crying for tomorrow to come when she could lavish all the pent-up love of the past four years on this dear unloved baby, their son.

Richly Blessed  4

1966-1968

"Fanny, come quickly!" Her husband's urgent call from the front door sent her dashing outdoors.

"What is it?" she asked in alarm when she saw Mark gazing skyward.

"Come, see the eagles? This pair of bald eagles must have claimed territory not far from here. Imagine having a pair build a nest in our area! I've seen them before, but I never dreamed this may be their territory."

Fanny was clueless as to why a pair of birds elicited such enthusiasm from her husband. "Oh," came her feeble response. She had been preparing clothes and the crib for their baby, and Mark thought she should be excited about a pair of birds?

Mark turned to his wife, giving her his full attention. He had learned much in four years of marriage, and her answer showed him she was not exactly happy to be called out of the house to see some birds. "What did I interrupt when I called you out?" he asked.

"Oh, Mark, I was making sure I had enough baby clothes and blankets for our baby. I'm so glad we have a crib and those few clothes I kept on hand for children when I baby-sat. I think we can make do until I know his size and can sew for him."

Mark kissed her flushed cheek. It was as he thought. Her mind was on one thing: their coming baby.

"Sorry to interrupt you," he apologized. "When I saw the eagles I wasn't thinking of what you might be doing. Having you to myself these past four years has probably made me pretty selfish. Having a baby is going to bring changes to our lives. I'm looking forward to these changes, but I'll have to remember your time will no longer be your own."

Fanny's face glowed. How she loved her understanding husband! "For sure, I'll try not to forget the most important person around here!" she teased. "Now why are these birds so important?" she asked innocently.

"I'll tell you later!" Mark laughed. "On with you!" He patted her shoulder and laughed again.

"I'll tell you on our way to get our son!" he called after her retreating figure, and chuckling to himself, he headed back to the barn to finish his morning's work. *Yes, life will be different for both of us.*

They had barely made it to the highway when Fanny said softly, "Tell me about the birds."

"Are you sure?" he questioned. "You wouldn't rather talk about our son?"

She laughed. "Of course. But I do need to know why you were so excited about the birds!"

"Bald eagles are special birds," Mark explained. "They choose high, secluded sites for their homes, and they build a nest there where they stay for life. Since we've just started seeing this pair, I'm guessing they're newly mated.

"I noticed them several times this summer and wondered if they were looking for a place to build a nest. If they have chosen a site around here, I wouldn't be surprised if it's the old oak tree on your father's farm. That tree is the tallest landmark for miles around. I'm going to scout it out as soon as the leaves are off. To have a new pair locate in our area is interesting, since I've heard pesticides are harming bald eagles and their eggs, and their population is dwindling across the United States.

"Another important fact to know is that eagles will benefit your farmer father," he said. "Even though their favorite food is fish, eagles also keep rodents at bay!

"But the primary reason I've been fascinated with the huge, graceful birds is that my favorite verse in the Bible talks about them. Isaiah 40:31 says, 'They that wait upon the LORD shall renew their strength; they shall mount up with wings as eagles; they shall run, and not be weary; and they shall walk, and not faint.' "

"That's beautiful," Fanny said. "Beautiful." Several more minutes passed before she spoke again. "It seems we've waited a long time for a baby of our own."

Mark squeezed her fingers wrapped around his. "I know. It's exciting, even though I know he's going to be a big responsibility. One thing I've been thinking about though is that caring for his physical needs and loving him now will probably be easy. But how will his handicaps affect him and us as he grows older?

He paused for a bit and then spoke again. "And you know, that brings me back to the eagles. There's another verse that says, 'As an eagle stirreth up her nest, fluttereth over her young, spreadeth abroad her wings, taketh them, beareth them on her wings: so the Lord alone did lead him.' The verse is referring to God's care of Israel, but we could apply it to ourselves. God will be with us and lead us each day in building a safe place for our baby. He will give us the strength for this responsibility if we ask for His help."

"Mark, what a beautiful thought. I'm glad you shared it with me. My heart is so full. God is so good to us." She raised her shining eyes to his and gripped his hand a little tighter. *A safe place!* She hugged the thought close to her heart. With God's help, she and Mark would provide the best home they could for their son.

The hearts of both of the young parents-to-be were pounding hard when they walked into Mrs. Sims' office and took seats in the waiting room.

"Mr. and Mrs. King?" the secretary asked as she rose to meet them. "Come with me," she smiled and led them down a hall to the door of a private room. Opening the door, she stepped back saying, "Go right in. I believe some-one is waiting to meet you."

A beautiful little red-haired boy sat in the middle of the floor with an orange ball beside him. Mark and Fanny felt frozen in place as they watched their son, the son they had been told was practically blind, swat the ball with his hand, then reach out for it as it rolled away.

"He can see! Your baby can see!" Mrs. Sims beamed as she scooped up Baby Boy O'Connor and handed him to his waiting parents.

"This little fellow is a miracle baby if I ever saw one. Take your time, and learn to know him. I will be back later."

Mrs. Sims closed the door behind her, leaving the new family alone.

"I doubt if the parents heard a word I said," she told her secretary. "Baby Boy O'Connor is one blessed baby."

Baby Connor did not protest the kisses or cuddles showered on him, but neither did he respond. "He'll change," Mark encouraged his wife. "Let's be thankful he isn't afraid of us."

"Look at his clothes! Socks, a diaper, and a T-shirt. That is all he is wearing! Poor dear little boy, how could anyone not want you?" As Fanny held her little curly-haired son in her arms, she marveled, "This is what my friends meant when they said, 'The minute I held my baby, we bonded.'"

"Andy James. I like the name we chose. He looks exactly like an Andy, doesn't he?" Fanny murmured as she kissed the top of his silky head and settled him into his daddy's arms.

That evening Mark asked, "Should I give my son his bath?"

"What?" Fanny sputtered, the question taking her by surprise. But if her husband wanted to bathe their baby, she would let him. It was fun to watch Mark give Andy his bath and encourage him to splash. To their astonishment Andy hit the water with both his little hands and splashed. Clapping his hands, he smacked the water again.

"Handicapped? This little chap is certainly not handicapped! He's not blind or abnormal in any way I can detect," Mark stated emphatically as he wrapped their son in a towel and handed him to his mother.

When they took Andy in for his one-year checkup the

doctor pronounced him completely normal. "Say a thank you to God," their doctor told them. "From what his report says, I was expecting to notice some progressive deterioration in his physical and mental abilities. I have found none. Give thanks to God is all I can say."

Andy thrived, growing steadily. His development kept pace with cousins close to his age, twin girls who lived nearby.

On June 26, 1968, the Kings received their final letter from the Child Welfare Board:

> Dear Mr. and Mrs. Mark King and Andy:
>
> This is a day you've looked forward to for some time—the final adoption. As far as the three of you are concerned, this only makes legal a relationship that has existed almost from the first day you took your son into your home.
>
> I have been pleased with the way you three have become a family, and I was happy to recommend that the adoption be made final.
>
> Very truly yours,
> Lorena Sims
> Executive Secretary
> Child Welfare Board

On July 3, 1968, the adoption of Andy James King was finalized.

"This is strange!" Mark stated as they read Andy's birth certificate for the first time. "There is no doctor's signature!" On questioning Mrs. Sims about it, she said, "It appears the delivering doctor did not expect the baby to live, and it obviously got overlooked until after he was discharged. God did give you a miracle baby!"

"Yes, we feel blessed," Mark agreed. "Richly blessed."

A Farewell and a Flood

5

1969

Affectionate, tenderhearted, three-year-old Andy loved living next door to Mark's parents. A close bond sprang up between the red-haired grandson and his feeble, aged grandfather. Andy started a daily ritual of eating his supper, then running out the door of their basement home, down the short sidewalk, and through the open arbor gate to see "my Dawdy." Each evening his beloved Dawdy was waiting for his arrival in his chair at the kitchen table.

"Dawdy! I'm here!" was the standard greeting Andy bestowed as he climbed up onto his lap and leaned contentedly against Dawdy's soft, tickly beard. "What do you have for me to eat?" This question always brought a wheezing chuckle from the elderly man as his grandson proceeded to eat whatever food Grandmother had saved back from their own supper. To Fanny's dismay, her son ate things he had trouble enjoying at home—like the crust on his bread or the skin on an apple. At Dawdy's he ate whatever he was given without one word of complaint.

Fanny was glad her son could brighten Dawdy's last days, but she worried about how his death would affect their son.

The time came sooner than they expected. One evening Andy could not eat fast enough. "I need to go see my

Dawdy," he kept saying. Finally his plate was clean, and he ran next door, but he stopped when he came to the porch steps. *Why was Dawdy in his outdoor rocker instead of sitting at the table indoors?*

"Dawdy?" he called but grew even more puzzled when all was silent. *Why doesn't Dawdy answer?* Andy's mind churned. He did not like this change of routine! When Dawdy finally reached out a shaky hand, Andy climbed contentedly onto his lap and said, "Dawdy, I'm here." He waited for the deep, rumbling chuckle he loved to hear as he leaned against his chest, but nothing came, except the slow rise and fall of wheezy breathing.

Andy sat quietly for a couple of minutes in the silence of the porch. He didn't like the difference. He could hear Grandmother clearing up the dishes when he remembered that he hadn't even had a taste of their supper! Things were not right!

Climbing down from Dawdy's lap, he ran back home. "Mama, Dawdy acts funny," he pouted.

Mark rose abruptly from the table where he and his wife were enjoying a quiet cup of coffee. As he started to speak, Grandmother's frantic call reached them. "Mark! Mark! Come quickly!"

Both knew the time they feared had come. Without saying a word, Fanny reached for their son as her husband went to help his mother.

The funeral was huge. Andy clung to his parents, not understanding why Dawdy didn't get out of his box bed. When his daddy tried to tell him, "Dawdy is in heaven," Andy couldn't comprehend it. He shook his head but didn't say a word. *What did Daddy mean? His Dawdy wasn't gone; he was sleeping right there!* Yet everything was mixed up. Nothing was right, and it frightened him. The only way Andy knew how to cope with his upside-down world was to draw back in silence. Because he seemed to quietly accept Dawdy's death, his parents did not realize the magnitude of the pain he held inside his tender, grieving heart.

Dawdy's body was buried between rain showers. The family was grateful to God for allowing the rain to let up for the burial. By late afternoon of the same day the rain fell without stopping. It rained all evening, and the community went to sleep with rain pounding on their rooftops. Water bounced out of spouting, creating miniature lakes and rivers through soggy yards. Local creeks were already swollen to capacity from the previous week's precipitation, and now they spilled over their banks.

Because darkness concealed the raging, rising waters boiling between the high rocky banks of Stoner Creek, the Kings went to sleep without a thought of danger. A car crept slowly across the water-covered bridge. *Whap, whap,* went the windshield wipers. *Whap, whap, whap.* The driver leaned over the steering wheel, but it was impossible to see out of the windshield that was being pummeled by rain. "Hope I'm in the middle of this bridge!" he muttered, gasping as the car swung a little bit sideways with the current. He clenched the steering wheel tighter and did not loosen his grip until he felt the front tires grip the blacktop. "Whew! Almost home!" He relaxed his grip as the car chugged uphill through the rain.

The culvert beneath the bridge was huge. Local children used it as a fun place to wade or a safe walkway under the busy road. Rushing water on the east side of the culvert had carved out a large swimming pool edged with shady, over-hanging tree branches. The Kings' property was situated on a high ridge above the southeast bank and followed the water's curve for another quarter mile through the woods.

Tonight, the culvert could not divert the torrent sweeping eastward. Water burst over the bridge and flooded the roadway, spilling into the strong current on the other side. Minutes after the car crossed the water-covered bridge, a grating, crashing roar mingled with the downpour as the bridge broke from its moorings. Rocks, torn loose by the water's strength, pounded the culvert until pieces of pavement on both sides were knocked off. The weakened rock walls holding the culvert were no match for the wall of surging water and rock. In another groaning, grinding moment, the steel culvert was wrenched away, leaving a deep, dangerous hole of swirling water separating one side of the road from the other.

Higher and higher the water crept through the dark, star-less night. It rose so high that it overflowed the steep bank bordering the Kings' property. It didn't take the rising water long to find the outdoor stairway to the basement house. Water trickled merrily down one step and then another until it pooled outside the entry door. Water seeped in through the locked door and inched across the floor to meet the steady stream of water flowing up and out of the inside floor drain.

At 5:00 a.m. Mark's inner alarm clock woke him. *Chore time!* He wanted to roll over and go back to sleep, but if he didn't get up, he would be late for work at the fencing shop next door. He swung his legs over the side of the bed, and his feet hit icy cold water.

"Fanny! There's water in our house!" he gasped in a loud whisper. His shocking words in the inky darkness brought panic to his wife, who sat bolt upright, ready to jump out of bed.

"Fanny, stay put. It feels like I'm standing in more than a foot of water!" Mark instructed as he sloshed to where their dresser stood. "Let me light the lamp so we can see what is going on."

"Hurry, Mark! Check Andy!" Alarm for their son made Fanny want to leap out of bed at that instant.

"I can't even find my clothes! They must be floating around somewhere in this water," Mark mumbled before his hand struck the lamp resting in its familiar place. Once the lamp blazed with light, they both gaped at the unbelievable sight that met their eyes. Water covered the entire floor, reaching as high as their mattress. He sputtered in disbelief when he located his wet clothes plastered against the partly submerged dresser.

Mark went to his son, who was fast asleep in his crib. *What if their little boy had awakened early and crawled over the crib side as he sometimes did? What if he had slipped into the water, and they hadn't found him in time?* Thanksgiving welled up within the parents' hearts as Daddy carried their sleeping son to the big bed and laid him safely with Mama.

"What a mess!" Fanny exclaimed to herself as she sloshed through the water in her husband's rubber boots to find dry clothes for her family. "At least the stove isn't ruined, and most stuff can be dried out. I guess I can face almost anything if both Andy and Mark are safe."

Early Years 6

1970-1976

"Mama, why can't I have a baby brother?" Andy asked when they left his twin cousins' place. "Alma and Anna don't need a new baby, but I do, 'cause there's only me!"

Fanny wanted to agree with his logic, but she knew it would not help. "Let's pray for a baby brother. Remember how Daddy and I told you we wanted a baby so much because we didn't have one?"

"And God had a sick little baby boy waiting for you, but you didn't even know it!" Andy rushed to finish the story he loved to help tell. "And it was me! And you prayed and prayed, and when you got me I wasn't even sick!

"Mama, I'm so glad I have a home and my own sweet mama and daddy," he solemnly informed her as she guided the horse trotting down the road toward home.

"Daddy and I are happy, too, that God gave us our very own baby boy." She shared a smile with her affectionate son.

"I'm going to pray every day for God to give me a baby brother."

"Daddy and I will pray with you," Fanny assured him.

"Maybe God already has a baby brother waiting for us,

and we don't know it yet!" Andy brightened.

Asking for a baby brother became a part of every nightly prayer. God did have another baby boy waiting to join the family, but to Andy it felt like a long time until God found one. Yet Andy did not forget his prayers. Months later, when baby Joshua arrived, five-year-old Andy ended his nightly prayer with, "Thank you, Jesus, for giving me a brother."

Andy dearly loved his little brother, but Joshua spent most of his time sleeping or lying listlessly on the couch. He had been born prematurely and his tiny body struggled to catch up so Joshua didn't need much entertainment in the early days.

One year later baby Joseph joined the family. "Mama, I never even prayed, and God had another baby waiting for us!" Andy remarked happily when they brought Joseph home. And with Joseph in the home, Andy had more opportunities to feel like a real big brother.

Joseph was a restless baby due to the drugs his birth mother had taken while carrying him. When summer arrived, Andy would pull his brothers around their small acreage in his wagon, keeping Joseph entertained. He never tired of this. On rainy days the wagon was brought inside, and Andy pretended to be the horse hauling his brothers around and around the kitchen table until Fanny thought he would wear a permanent path on the cement floor.

Andy took seriously his responsibility to help keep his brothers happy. When he learned one morning he would be going to the dentist to get his tooth pulled, he thought of a way to make Daddy forget about going. "Daddy," he said firmly as he rubbed his chin, copying his father's mannerism, "Mama needs me at home to pull the wagon. I don't think I can go to Dr. Wolf's today."

"Well, son," his dad's eyes crinkled at the corners as he, too, stroked his chin. "I bought something for you that I thought you could show Dr. Wolf. It's in my pocket, but if you don't want to go to the dentist, I can take it back to the store."

"Oh, no, Dad! I think I will want it." He quickly changed his mind about staying home. *Daddy bought me something from a store?* Excitement mounted as Daddy reached into his pocket.

"Since you have learned to tell time without even going to school, Mama and I thought you could use this," Daddy said as he pulled out a shiny silver pocket watch. Andy's smile grew bigger and bigger. He forgot all about getting a tooth pulled as he cradled the watch in his hands.

"My own?" he asked in breathless wonder.

"Yes, son. Your very own watch."

"Daddy! The fob even has a horse on it!" Throwing his arms around his daddy's neck, he said, "Thank you, Daddy. I'm so glad I have a home and such a sweet mama and daddy."

"Are you going to show it to Dr. Wolf?" Daddy asked as he swallowed the lump forming in his throat.

"For sure, I will show it to Dr. Wolf!"

Once they arrived at the dentist's office and left the safety of their buggy, Andy's dread of visiting the dentist returned. Clutching his watch tightly in his hands did not chase away the rising fear in his chest. As they walked up the dentist office steps, he suddenly thought of something. "Daddy," he said emphatically. "I'm not having anything to do with a wolf!"

"Well, son," Daddy chuckled, opening the door. "We are here now. Remember what you wanted to show Dr. Wolf?" When they were ushered directly into Room 2, he helped his son onto the chair and encouraged, "If you hold your watch it will be ready to show the doctor." Andy obeyed and even relaxed a little as the dentist's assistant laid his chair back and gave him a candy-flavored stick to hold between his teeth.

"That is quite a watch fob you have there, isn't it, young man? Where did you get it?" Dr. Wolf asked when he entered the room and saw what his patient was holding. Andy looked up to explain when the dentist said, "Don't tell me yet! I need you to open your mouth while I get my toothbrush out," and as he talked, he extracted the tooth without his young patient knowing it was being done.

Keen disappointment flashed across Andy's face when Dr. Wolf said, "I'm finished, young man. Now you can tell me about your watch fob."

"My tooth's already out? When did you do it?" Andy asked in confusion as the men chuckled, and he forgot all about telling Dr. Wolf about his watch.

Andy started school the winter he turned seven. Since their Amish schoolhouse was filled to capacity, Andy began first grade at the local public school where several of his older cousins were also attending. For the first time in his life, Andy's innocent trust in people was rudely destroyed. He quickly found out that being adopted made other children not like him. It seemed that being adopted made him a nobody.

"Don't sit with me," a third-grade boy hissed as Andy got on the bus at the end of the third school day. "He's that adopted King kid," the bully sneered as Andy stumbled blindly on. Tears swam in his eyes. *Why did he say that? Mama said being adopted was special! He makes it sound mean.* His heart ached as he struggled to hold back the sob trying to escape.

"Andy, here!" Cousin Josiah's familiar voice guided him to a refuge. "Don't pay attention to those bullies. They're troublemakers," he said, trying to comfort his little cousin.

Andy kept wiping his eyes on his shirtsleeve. "But Josiah, what's wrong with being adopted?" he was finally able to ask. His eleven-year-old cousin shrugged, not knowing how to answer. *What could he say?* The older cousins had always shielded their special redheaded cousin from the unkind remarks that floated around him. It angered Josiah when people spoke disrespectfully about being adopted. Andy was a whole lot nicer than some of the other boys his age.

Josiah couldn't bear seeing Andy's forlorn, tearstained face staring straight ahead. Seeing his cousin's left eyelid jump made him feel miserable. *Why did English[1] children have to be so cruel? It wasn't fair.* Leaning close to Andy, he whispered in his ear, "Listen, cousin, stick with me when school's out. I'll wait for you each evening before we get on the bus. Okay?"

Andy brightened and nodded, but when the bus stopped at his lane and he walked down the aisle, the bully hissed,

---

[1] Amish people often use the term *English* to refer to anyone who is not Amish.

"Dirty mud clod!" and stuck out his foot, tripping Andy. Josiah sucked in his breath, but let it out when Andy caught himself before falling to the floor and got safely off the bus.

The stinging taunts followed Andy off the bus; they followed him up his lane. They stuck with him as he passed Dawdy's house. "I wish Dawdy were here," he sobbed as he ran on to his own home with the taunts ringing in his ears.

Andy could hear Joseph whimpering as he entered the house. Peeking into the living area, he saw Mama's eyes closed as she hummed softly in the rocking chair, trying to get fussy little Joseph to sleep. Andy quietly hung up his jacket, put his lunch containers by the sink and went to change his school clothes.

Mama looks tired. I won't bother telling her, he decided. *It might make her sad, and I don't want my sweet mama sad.* When he came out of his bedroom, all traces of tears had vanished.

Though Andy never shared the incident with his parents, the cruel hurt lodged deeply in his sensitive heart. He began to notice anything that was hurting, and caring for the less fortunate became his mission.

Grandpa Yoder, Fanny's father, became a central figure in Andy's life the summer before he started second grade. Andy loved to go to his farm and learn how to care for Grandpa's cows, pigs, and chickens. They had goats and a pony at home, but the few chores never provided enough work to keep him busy. Since Grandpa and Grandma Yoder lived only two and a half miles from the Kings, Andy could ride his bicycle over to help with chores. As the summer work increased, he often stayed a week at a time on the farm. Since Mark was tied up with his day job, and Grandpa's farm work never ended, the arrangement benefited everyone. Having an energetic youngster willing to tackle jobs was a big boost to Andy's grandparents.

That summer Andy became fascinated with the bald eagles nesting on Grandpa's farm. One day Grandpa Yoder took Andy to see the eagle nest, the same nest that Andy's father had suspected was there years before. Nearly eight years had passed now since the day Mark had called Fanny out of the house to see the eagles soaring overhead, the day they first brought Andy home.

"My dad likes the eagles, and so do I," Andy stated as they walked around the alfalfa field abuzz with working bees. Late morning breezes made the hay field, nearly ready for cutting, fragrant with the scent of ripe, sweet alfalfa. "I wish they would let us come close enough to see their white head feathers."

"There's one!" Grandpa pointed, and together they stopped and watched the huge bird float on the wind currents high above them. "Now, look at him through these binoculars." Grandpa said, adjusting the lens before handing them to his grandson.

"Wow, Grandpa! You can really see their black and white feathers!" Seeing the magnificent eagle close up stirred something inside Andy. He stood in silence gazing at the glistening eagle with its wide wingspan and white wingtips and head. Suddenly, the eagle dived straight down, its wings plastered to its sides. Andy's arms tingled; he gripped the binoculars tighter. He held his breath and was sure he heard the wind whistle with the speed of the falling bird. *Would the eagle crash into the ground?* Then he saw the streaking eagle lift its wings and level out effortlessly before flapping upward into the clear blue sky.

"Grandpa!" he panted, unable to say more.

For a time the two tramped through the woods in silence, awed by the spectacular scene they had witnessed. Andy walked as if in a dream, and only when Grandpa touched his arm did he return to the present.

"We have the tallest oak tree in the area," Grandpa explained. "Eagles need to nest high above everything, and that is why they chose this spot. It's an old, old tree with thick, spreading branches that can hold the eagle's huge nest. Can you see it? If we get closer you won't be able to see as well as we can from here. Use your binoculars and look at the top."

"All I see is leaves," Andy answered in disappointment.

"Let me try," Grandpa said, taking the binoculars. He soon gave them back. "You're right. The tree is too leafy to see the nest. Now that you know where the tree is, you can come back this fall after the leaves have fallen and see it."

"Grandpa, did you ever see an eagle dive before?"

"Yes, Andy, but each time it happens, it is a marvel. God made everything good, His Word tells us, and that certainly includes the eagle."

Andy's heart tightened. He longed to understand the God who made the beautiful eagle. "Even me?" The doubtful question made Grandpa look sharply at his grandson.

"Even you. Don't forget, Andy, His Word tells us 'thou hast covered me in my mother's womb.' That means God knew all about you and took care of you before you were born.

God had a home waiting for you when the time was right."

Andy slipped his hand into Grandpa's big warm one, then asked in a small, strained voice. "Where, Grandpa, where does it say that?" He felt his left eyelid fluttering. He hated when it did that, but Mama said it was "just the way it was."

"In the Bible, my boy. Psalm 139:13 tells us those precious words." Grandpa had a hard time keeping his voice steady. He wondered what trials little Andy had already faced. Was he being ridiculed in school?

Grandpa knew that it wasn't just school where Andy could have heard hurtful things. He thought back to a conversation he had overheard recently during church lunch when a young father had been talking about his sons' misdeeds.

"I can't understand why they did it! Now if they had been adopted like Andy King, I would have expected it."

Angered at the injustice of the man's words, he, Noah Yoder, had wanted to lash out and set the man straight. He had wanted to shame him, put him in his place, and stand up for his grandson. Immediately, however, Grandpa Yoder recognized the sin in his attitude. No, he would need to let it go. He would pray that the man would see the damage he was doing to both himself and his boys for having such a wrong attitude toward adopted children.

Andy kept repeating the Bible reference in his mind as he and Grandfather trudged home in silence. *I will have Dad show me,* he determined. *I want to see the Bible verse myself.*

Each year that Andy attended public school proved to

be another year of facing taunts and unfair treatment from some of the older students. Being adopted labeled him as unintelligent, unable to learn or play games well. Being adopted meant his mother had hated him and given him away, or that his mother had been really, really bad and had wanted nothing to do with her bad baby. Being adopted meant his blood was bad, and no one wanted to trade lunch items with Andy for fear they would become tainted . . . all these were things he was taunted with at school.

Yet the accusations did not cause Andy to retaliate. Instead, he became a quiet, conscientious boy, careful with both his words and actions. Many good things happened at school and many children befriended him, but the stigma of adoption spoiled his joy of learning.

One noon hour, fourth-grade Andy and his fifth-grade cousin, Dan, were helping to play round-table Ping-Pong. Both boys played the game well since they had played Ping-Pong with their friends and cousins even before they were old enough to attend school. Competition always ran strong in these games, so you had to learn quickly in order to stay in the game.

"Hey, Dan!" an older schoolmate shouted as he watched Andy and Dan, the final players in the game, battle with each other. *Whap! Whap!* The ball danced from one side of the table to the other with each boy returning the spins or spikes without missing one hit. "Come on," the classmate sneered, jerking his hand toward Andy. "Get him out! Andy's just a nobody!"

"Why do you say that?" Dan shot back. "He is, too, somebody!" and the ball continued to dance back and forth. Andy loved his cousin for defending him in front of all their classmates. For once the jabs did not destroy the rush of gladness he felt in having Dan's support.

His heart carried the glow all afternoon. It stayed with him as he rode the bus home, and its embers fanned brighter as he walked up the familiar lane. Suddenly he ached with intense love for his dear home and parents. *His home!* He drank in the beautiful trees shading the yard and Mom's flowerbeds—a riot of reds and yellows. He looked toward the buggy barn where the frolicking goats and horses always seemed glad to see him. *I love living here! I love the family God gave me.* Conflicting thoughts swept over him, and he stopped in his tracks, trying to figure out why he had so many empty, mixed-up feelings. It always felt like he had a dark hole inside, that something was missing, that he needed to reach out and grab something. He didn't know how to fill up the emptiness—the emptiness of not knowing where he came from.

Maybe I don't love Dad and Mom enough, he agonized, but he didn't know how to love them any more than he already did. There was no doubt in his mind that his parents, his grandparents, and his cousins all loved and accepted him. He didn't want them to feel bad or think he wasn't happy, so he kept his troubling questions locked inside his heart.

Yet as he grew older, the questions grew stronger. *Why did my birth mother give me away? Does she ever feel sad and want to see me? Do I look like her? Or do I look like my father? Do I even have a father? Maybe my father is a terrible person in prison. Maybe I am one of "those children" the schoolchildren whisper that I am. What if I am? Would I want to know if I actually had bad blood like they say?*

Among all his other questions, that one haunted him the most. He shuddered at the fear of it being true. *It can't be! I can't be one of "those children."*

Besides being adopted, Andy felt like he was different from his cousins in other ways. They all trapped muskrats in Stoner Creek, but he couldn't bear to hurt the animals. Seeing the drowned animals caught in steel traps made him sick to his stomach. The first time he saw his dad skin one, he almost went crazy. "Get it out of here!" Andy cried in horror, and Dad had moved to a place where Andy wasn't watching. He hated not being able to go trapping with his father like his cousins did with their dads, but he couldn't. *At least Dad understands.* He consoled himself with that knowledge, but it hurt to be different.

Even on butchering day, Andy had different jobs than the other boy cousins. He had to do things that did not involve seeing the actual killing or cutting up the meat. Andy longed to be a part of the men's activities, but his stomach could not handle the blood and raw meat. If he didn't want to get sick, he had to stay away from such sights and smells. *Did I get this from my mother or my father, or am I just dumb?* Andy wondered. He wished for an answer, to be able to say, "My dad could never butcher. Guess I am like him."

The woods on Grandpa Yoder's farm became a haven for Andy. Though there was a small woods and creek at home where he and his younger brothers hunted mushrooms, Andy had no privacy there, since Joshua and Joseph used the whole woods for their playground.

His cousins never hunted in Grandpa's woods, so the

woods seemed to belong to him. Andy couldn't bring himself to talk to the other boys of his fascination with the eagles or his forest friends. Squirrels scampered to meet him, searching for the nuts or seeds he hid under bushes. His patience won over some of the small feathered birds that nested on nearby limbs, and they would hop close to Andy fearlessly. He had even chanced to see a field mouse dart out and grab some of the scattered seeds.

Only Grandpa Yoder and his parents knew about this part of Andy's life. Both had sensed his need for a private place to call his own. Andy whooped in joy when he received both a pair of binoculars and a bird book for his eleventh birthday. Hours of free time were spent learning from the birds or simply enjoying nature's solace.

Preacher's Son 7

"**C**hurch will be different today," Dad King explained to his oldest son as they drove to church. "Do you remember that two weeks ago Bishop Mose announced we should pray about ordaining another minister?"

"Yes," Andy replied. This was something new. He had never been in an ordination service before.

"Following the communion service this afternoon, there will be preparation for the ordination tonight," his father continued. "Remember to behave and be quiet. It will be a long day."

Preaching always lasted until two o'clock on communion day, with various visiting ministers taking part. At noon, Bishop Mose and the visiting minister who would speak on Christ's suffering rose to go eat. This was the signal Andy had been waiting for. Lunchtime had arrived! His stomach was feeling absolutely hollow. He could already taste the thick slices of homemade bread covered with sandwich meat or spread with peanut butter shmear[1] or jam.

I'm going to take meat, he decided. *Yum! Meat sandwiches, pickles, and cookies . . .* His daydreaming was interrupted

---

[1] A spread made with peanut butter, marshmallow cream, and pancake syrup, a common part of the meal after Amish church services.

when the men on his bench rose to file out.

Preaching continued through the noon hour. One bench of people at a time would leave the meeting to eat. The people ate quickly and returned to their seats so the people on the next bench could leave. After everyone had eaten and sat down again, the visiting minister spoke about Christ's suffering. "Long before Jesus was born, Isaiah prophesied that Jesus would be despised and rejected of man," he began. "Even Peter, Jesus' own disciple, denied Him, and the others fled."

Rejected? Andy sat up straighter. *Jesus was rejected?* He had just recently learned that word. In fact, he'd heard it whispered about him. "His mother rejected him at birth." Not being wanted—that must be what rejection was. He felt that at school, too, when students didn't want to play with him or sit with him. Rejection . . . Andy finally had a name for what caused the black hole, the thing that set him apart. Yet having a name for what he felt didn't seem to solve anything.

He frowned in concentration. He didn't remember ever hearing someone preach about rejection before. *Guess I haven't listened very much,* he admitted and turned his attention back to the words the minister was now reading from the Bible, hoping more would be said. Suddenly he was glad he could understand the German reading, glad that Dad and Mom always used German at home when they read the Bible and prayed, instead of using English as some of the other families did.

"He was wounded for our transgressions . . . with his stripes we are healed. All we like sheep have gone astray . . . the

LORD hath laid on him the iniquity of us all." The words from the Scripture reading kept going around in his mind. He couldn't understand their meaning exactly, but he pondered them as he watched the church members taking a piece of bread and a sip of wine and heard Bishop Mose say, " 'This do in remembrance of me.' " He remembered Mama explaining that as they drank the wine and ate the bread, they thought of what Jesus had suffered on the cross.

He felt older today and enjoyed singing the final song of the communion service. Bishop Mose's voice sounded unusually serious to Andy as his voice rose and fell in prayer. "O heavenly Father, we praise and thank thee for thy inexpressibly great grace and thy unfathomably great love which thou hast shown us through Jesus Christ our Lord and Saviour—Thou, O Lord Jesus Christ, who hast brought and redeemed us with thy holy and precious merits on the cross, on which thou didst let thy holy body be broken and thy holy blood be shed, and didst become a pure sacrifice, holy and perfect, for us sinners . . ."[2]

While eating supper, Andy noticed that mainly visitors and children were eating. He and his cousins ate without talking. Everyone else was either silent or talking in hushed tones, and he knew it had to do with the ordination service that evening. He did not realize the heavy burden resting on the hearts of the faithful brothers and sisters in the local congregation. He was too young to understand the seriousness of being the one God would call as minister or the question burning in each brother's mind: *Who*

[2] Prayer taken from Our Heritage, Hope, and Faith, a collection of English translations of German prayers, songs, etc., p. 218.

will be chosen? Surely not I! It will be someone more quali-fied, but who?

The service resumed, and Bishop Mose announced, "The time has come for you as a congregation to nominate a qualified brother to be a minister. Sisters will use the door on my right, and brethren, the door on my left. Enter the doors one at a time to give your nomination. The ministers in those rooms will record the names given. Anyone receiving three or more votes will be in the lot."

Andy watched attentively as two lines were formed, the women on the right and the men on the left. He watched as one person at a time entered the closed doors. *Swish-open. Swish-click-shut.* The two doors were hardly closed before they opened and repeated the cycle. It seemed the longer Andy sat watching the doors and people file through, the harder the bench became.

Finally the last person exited the side doors and sat down. Only the ministers remained behind the closed doors. Someone cleared his throat. Someone else coughed, and Andy squirmed, trying to stretch his legs. Dad glanced at him, giving him a faint smile. Andy knew his dad must be tired of sitting, too, and he sat up straighter, copying his dad's ramrod posture. Suddenly, one of the front room doors opened and the ministers filed in.

A visiting minister stood and said, "We will now read how a minister's wife is to conduct herself. In 1 Timothy 3:11 we read, 'Even so must their wives be grave, not slan-derers, sober, faithful in all things.' "

Fanny glanced over at her husband and son sitting so at-tentively. *My Mark could be a minister, but I would never qualify as a minister's wife.* Inwardly she sighed with relief. *I don't have to worry; I would never be included. I do try to be faithful in all things, but I know I talk too much, and I struggle with having the love I ought toward everyone.*

Bishop Mose stood before the congregation and solemnly looked over the sea of faces. It seemed as if his piercing, saintly eyes could see into the hearts of each one sitting there. The room became deathly quiet. A holy hush surrounded them as they waited to hear the names of those whom the church felt were qualified for this office.

"We have the names of three brethren: Harvey Raber, Mark King, and Marlin Fisher," Bishop Mose announced. "On the table I am placing three books. One of them has a slip of paper at page 770. The books have been rearranged by four ministers, and I will shuffle them again. God is the only one who knows which book holds the slip of paper. May His will be done."

Bishop Mose picked up the three identical Ausbund songbooks and laid them on the table. Fanny clutched three-year-old sleeping Joseph so tightly he started to whimper. *Not Mark!* her heart cried. *Let it be one of the others!*

"We will have these three brethren come and take the front bench while their wives sit on the bench behind them," Bishop Mose instructed, giving Fanny no time to collect her thoughts. Her sister-in-law came and took both Joshua and Joseph. There was nothing she could do but follow the other two women and take a seat behind Mark.

Andy sat glued to his seat. *Dad, a minister?* He was grateful his dad had squeezed his hand before moving to the front bench. His heart thudded, and his eyelid wouldn't hold still when he noticed his mom's ashen face and bowed head.

Bishop Mose continued, "Now let us follow the same way Matthias was chosen. Acts 1:24-25 reads, 'And they prayed, and said, Thou, Lord, which knowest the hearts of all men, show whether of these [three] thou hast chosen, that he may take part of this ministry . . .' " He picked up the books again and shuffled them several times before placing them in a row on the table beside him. Each songbook was tied with a string, and all looked the same to Andy. *How would his dad know which one to take?*

"Let us kneel and pray." The congregation knelt in silent prayer for several minutes before rising and standing in reverent silence for another minute. Bishop Mose then prayed audibly.

"God in heaven, who knowest the hearts of these brethren and the one thou hast chosen to preach thy Word, we pray, fill him with thy Holy Spirit. Give him understanding of thy holy Scriptures. Make him strong and steadfast. Fill his heart with love and compassion for the church and its members. Make him a light to lead and give guidance. Grace his lips with kindness to rebuke and correct when needed. Bless his companion that she, too, will feel the call, and support her husband in the work of Christ's kingdom. Amen."

The audible prayer gave Fanny courage to pray silently, "Yes, Lord, I am willing to do whatever Mark and I are asked to do. It is so hard to think about, but thy will be done."

Mark, too, struggled with surrender to God's will, but when Bishop Mose closed his prayer, he knew that God was leading Him to choose the last book. He also knew that whatever the outcome, God's grace would be enough.

Harvey Raber got up and took the middle book, then sat back down. Suspense heightened. A baby cried. Fanny watched as her Mark, gifted, gentle, and God-fearing, took the last book without hesitating. Then Amos Fisher stood and took the remaining book before he, too, sat back down. It was the first book their bishop had placed.

The room was deathly quiet; the congregation leaned forward on their backless benches as Bishop Mose walked over and stood in front of Harvey, who sat with bowed head, holding the book he had chosen. Bishop Mose took the book, untied the string, and opened the book to page 770. Slowly he closed the book and returned it to the table behind him. Harvey was not the one God had chosen.

Fanny's chest tightened. She clasped her sweating hands as the string was untied from her husband's book. Suddenly she felt a great peace settle within her heart. She felt God's presence as clearly as if He had touched her with a tangible touch of divine grace. A tear trickled down Fanny's face as Mark's songbook was opened. Bishop Mose stopped, and his hand trembled as he withdrew a slip of paper from the book and looked at Mark's bowed head before reciting the first part of Acts 1:26.

" 'And they gave forth their lots; and the lot fell upon . . .' " Mose paused, and instead of continuing the verse with the name of Matthias, he said, "Mark King, the servant God has chosen.

"We will now read the second verse of the 'Lob'[3] song."

---

[3] The *Lob* song was sung at the beginning of every church service.

Open the mouth of thy servants, Lord,
And give them wisdom also,
That they may rightly speak thy Word
Which encourages a devout life,
And serves to glorify thee,
Give us a desire for such nourishment;
This is our petition.[4]

Soft weeping could be heard from the women's side. Brethren wiped eyes and wept inwardly for the responsibility now resting on the young shoulders of their church brother. Mark stood in front of them now, answering with a firm, "I do" and "I will," the questions the bishop asked him.

Fanny could not staunch her tears until she heard the ageless blessing prayed, "The Lord make His face to shine upon you, and give you peace." The words lodged deep in her heart, giving her courage to face the changes that were ahead for them as a couple and a family.

Dad, a minister? Who will I sit with in church now? Andy sat alone on the hard church bench beside the big empty space Dad had left. He felt almost the same as he had when he had started attending school for the first time—fearful, deserted, and wishing he could go home where all remained familiar and safe. *Will the church boys still like me?* he wondered. *Will I be expected to act differently since Dad is now a minister?* His heart throbbed with anxiety of the unknown.

---

[4] Words taken from *Our Heritage, Hope, and Faith,* p. 223.

Spared!

1977

"Andy!" Dad called from the entrance of the buggy barn when he saw his son jump off his bike at the house. "Come see something!"

Mark watched his son hop off his well-worn bike and kick at the kickstand once, twice, three times before it held. "For sure, this ought to be fun," he chuckled as his son entered the shop and stopped in front of a brand new, single-speed blue Schwinn bicycle just his size.

"Dad!" The whoop that rang through the barn swelled the love in Mark's heart until he thought he couldn't contain it. "Where did you get it? Is it for me?"

"Yes, son, it belongs to you!"

"Thanks, Dad, thanks! You are the greatest dad ever! I love you!" Andy poured out his thanks, not even aware he had said, "I love you." He had said those words frequently when he was younger, but now he deemed them too childish for an almost-graduated fifth grader.

"I won this bike through a drawing at work," Dad explained. "It's yours. I hope you enjoy it!"

Being able to ride a new bike to school the last week before vacation was a tonic for the young adopted boy who had endured many hurts through five grades of school.

No one else in the entire elementary school owned a new Schwinn bicycle. The bright blue bicycle gleamed like a jewel among the well-ridden bicycles parked in the bike rack. Envy ran rampant, but no one dared make snide remarks. Andy King's name and a picture of the prized bicycle were even posted in the weekly newspaper. Teachers congratulated him, younger students clustered around the bike rack, and over a hundred pairs of eyes followed him when he left the schoolyard.

Saturday morning dawned with a fine, wispy fog hanging in the air. *Hope it turns nice for our school picnic today*, Andy thought as he wheeled his bicycle out of the buggy barn and up to the house so he could deliver a letter for Mom as soon as breakfast was finished.

It feels as if I hardly need to peddle! I love my new bike! he thought as he sped toward home after delivering the letter to the neighbors. He grinned as he pictured himself coasting down the road with his feet straight out, peddles turning like windmills, the momentum making him go faster and faster until he would rise off the ground and sail like an eagle through the air.

Andy was so busy imagining this extraordinary flight that he failed to notice how fast he was going up their lane until he hit wet grass and started sliding sideways. His back tire struck a small tree at the corner of the house, sending his bicycle spinning in the opposite direction while he flew headfirst into their brick basement wall. Blood gushed from his head wound, but not one scratch marred his new bicycle.

"Maybe you should stay home from the picnic," Mom suggested as she cleaned up the blood, worried that the impact might have done more than it presently appeared.

"Please, Mom. I won't play running games unless I feel like it," Andy begged. "I'll never get to go to the public school picnic again." *Or ride my new bicycle to one,* he wanted to add, but didn't.

"That is true. This is your last year in public school. Do be careful, and come right home if your head starts hurting," Mom admonished.

That fall Andy started sixth grade in their one-room Amish school. Before the week was over, he discovered that he did enjoy learning! He couldn't wait for school to begin each day. He loved his Amish teacher, and he loved being in a classroom with only Amish children. Life brightened, and he experienced a happiness he hadn't experienced the first five years of grade school.

One fall morning as Andy got ready to leave for school, his mother reminded him, "You have a doctor's appointment today. I'll be at the schoolhouse at noon to pick you up, and you can eat your lunch on the way to the doctor."

Biking to school wasn't necessary as their Amish school was just around the corner, but the big boys always biked. Today, though, Andy decided to walk with his little brothers who were in grades one and two. Andy loved his younger brothers as much as he had when they joined the family, but the difference in their ages created varied interests, and they seldom did things together.

This morning his brothers felt important as they tried to stretch their short legs to match their big brother's long stride. Andy grinned as he noticed that their steps were more like jumps. He shortened his step, and his heart swelled with thankfulness in knowing his brothers were spared the misery he went through while attending public school.

At noon dismissal Andy exited the school and climbed on the buggy seat beside his mother. "I'm starving!" He grinned as he opened his lunch bucket and sniffed the two thick, homemade sandwiches filled with leftover roast beef and pickles. A fried berry pie and an apple completed his lunch. His stomach rumbled as he took a big bite.

"Yum! You pack the best lunches, Mom," Andy said. He leaned back to enjoy his lunch and the swaying rhythm of their buggy as the horse trotted steadily down the smooth paved road. The metallic *clip-clop* of Shadow's shoes against the blacktop picked up speed as they started down the short hill. Andy was glad his side curtain was rolled up, so he could be prepared for the "swoosh" of oncoming cars. It seemed they passed at a tremendous rate of speed, and he liked knowing if one was coming. Mom kept her side curtain tightly closed because she felt safer that way, but he was glad she let him have his side open.

Here comes one, he thought as he watched a car approach as they neared the bottom of the hill. At the same time, the elegant brick house and outbuildings on Mom's side of the road caught his eye. Craning his neck, Andy leaned forward to look out the front window at the artistic landscaping and the winding, low brick fence surrounding the property.

Honk! Screech! Boom! A tremendous jolt threw him forward. The roar of a racing car motor, splintering wood, clang of metal, and Shadow's shrill scream of panic barely penetrated Andy's brain as he was slammed forward into the buggy's windshield, then tossed against the roof top and thrown unhurt in a heap on top of his mother. Their mangled buggy lay on its side with two wheels spinning madly in the air.

Shadow! Their mare's strangled screams rent the air. He could see her lying on her side, struggling to get up, but her bridle was thrown back over her head, pulling her mouth wide open. He had to help her! In his own panic he did not think to see if his mother was hurt. The loud cries of the strangled mare were all that registered.

Scrambling out of the buggy proved harder than it looked. By the time Andy managed to escape his prison, Shadow had untangled herself and was galloping up the road toward home with her reins trailing behind.

She's going to hurt herself! I have to catch her! Andy thought as he raced up the road after their mare.

If Andy had looked back he would have seen an oncoming car stop beside their overturned buggy. He would have seen the dazed driver who hit them stand beside the wreckage wringing his hands and crying, "I didn't see them! I came up over the hill and there they were!"

Andy also missed seeing the owners of the brick house race out to the smashed buggy. He did not realize the sheriff and ambulance were already on their way, and he had no idea that his mother was lying on her right side, moaning in pain. The thin, splintered buggy side had offered no protection from the hard brick wall against which she was thrown. She had borne the brunt of the impact when the buggy overturned.

Andy was still trying to catch up with their horse when

the ambulance turned on its siren and headed for the hospital with its unconscious passenger. He didn't even hear the eerie wail drifting over their peaceful Amish settlement, because at that very moment he caught up with Shadow.

Since the schoolhouse was nearby, Andy tied the horse there and went inside to tell the teacher what had happened. He asked if one of the older boys would call the vet and have him look at Shadow.

"I'll have one of them do that right now," Teacher Martha assured him. "How is your mom?" *Mom!* Andy panicked. He hadn't given his mother a thought.

"I'm going right back," he stammered. "I had to catch Shadow." For the first time since the accident, he remembered his mother. Racing back to the accident site, he found his mother nowhere around and the buggy being loaded onto a trailer.

"Where's Mom?" he asked Duff, the local sheriff.

"She was taken to the hospital and is in good hands," Duff assured the distraught boy. "Someone went to tell your father and take him to the hospital, so he's probably with her now." That added information did not help Andy feel better. *His mom, hurt? How badly was she injured?* he agonized.

Duff could tell that Mark King's boy was upset, and he didn't blame him. "Tell me what happened," he said. Andy calmed down a bit. He was relieved to talk to someone about the accident.

"Tell you what," said the big-hearted sheriff. "I'm finished up here and haven't had lunch. Come with me, and I'll buy you a sandwich."

"You go in first." Duff stepped back as he held the

restaurant door. "Let's see what people will say when they see you are with me! I bet they'll say, 'That boy is in trouble!' " The sheriff's eyes crinkled in laughter as they entered the restaurant. Sure enough, the restaurant grew quiet as people stopped talking to take in the unusual sight of big Sheriff Duff escorting a scared-looking Amish boy to a table.

Duff winked at him, and Andy relaxed. The sheriff proved an interesting lunch companion as they ate french fries and hot fish sandwiches. Conversation resumed in the restaurant, but the entire time they ate their lunch, Andy was aware of the curious glances sent his way.

Sheriff Duff took him home then, dropping him off at the end of his lane. When Andy arrived, he found that he was the only one at home. Even his grandmother, who lived next door, had gone away. Andy paced the house and the yard. Even when his brothers returned from school, he could not stop worrying about his mother.

Mark arrived home just before supper to find three frightened boys at home alone. "Mom will be fine," he reassured his sons. As Andy heard the welcome words, the tightness in his chest dissipated, and he could finally breathe freely.

Fanny remained in the hospital for three days while the doctors monitored her for internal injuries. After she was released, it took six weeks until her side was no longer sore and she felt able to do a full day's work.

Andy did all he could to help Mom as she recuperated. *What if she had been badly hurt? What if she had died?* He shuddered. He loved his mother so much. "Please, God, don't take my mother from me," became his nightly plea as she recovered.

Teen Years 9

1978-1983

Snow fell in abundance the winter Andy turned thirteen. Temperatures dipped below freezing and stayed there, making it possible for children, youth, and even adults to congregate opposite the King residence for sled rides down the steep slope of Cemetery Hill.

Some of the young men built ramps on the sledding trails. The drop-off at the end of a ramp left the rider suspended in midair before he hit the trail with a "swoosh" and shot like a bullet across the bottomland of Stoner Creek.

On the other side of Cemetery Hill, close to the road, was flatland that made a perfect spot for skating when it was flooded. By plugging the drainage tile in late fall, the locals had allowed the area to flood, turning it into what was now a good-sized skating pond. Skating weather was well into its second week when sixteen-year-old Lester Mast approached Mark.

"Some of us want to build a portable shanty on skids to use at the skating pond. May we build it in your buggy barn?"

Mark readily consented. "It will be good to have a place to change skates," he told the boys.

Early on Saturday morning a group of boys met at the

King barn. By mid-afternoon the finished shanty was being pulled by ropes to the skating pond.

"Stay away from those weeds," Lester panted as the boys neared the pond. "It never freezes well by the drain, so we don't want to put it there. If we park our shanty on the rise, it should be safe when it thaws."

The winter weather continued. Friday nights found both the sledding slope and skating pond packed with both Amish and their non-Amish neighbors.

One night a fast-skating neighbor was "it" in the game of rink tag.

"Can't catch me!" Johnny Yoder taunted him as he whizzed and dodged around other skaters who were not playing tag. The closer the fast skater came to catching Johnny, the more energy Johnny put into evading his pursuer. In a desperate attempt to put distance between them, he whipped around in a tight circle near the pond's edge, forgetting about the tough, treacherous weeds frozen in the ice. His skate blade caught in the weeds. His feet flew up in the air. *Smack!* The back of his head slammed against the ice. Johnny landed squarely on his back, unmoving, knocked out cold.

"I'll get help!" Ray Miller shouted. "I have my bike right here!" So saying, he skated to the fence where he had parked his bike. Stepping from the rink, he slipped his figure skates over the pedals and raced for help.

Johnny suffered a severe concussion and remained in the hospital a day and a half. The accident put a damper on the winter's remaining fun, reminding everyone how easily it could have ended in tragedy.

That spring Grandpa Yoder turned the plowing over to Andy. *I couldn't have a better job!* Andy whistled contentedly as he walked behind the three horses pulling in unison. Looking behind, he watched the single plow cutting a thin ribbon of rich black soil. The musky smell of damp earth mingled well with spring's scents of budding trees. Rafts of early white and lavender crowfoot blossoms carpeted the woods along the field.

A female American redstart flitted from branch to branch, looking for insects, while a yellow warbler trilled joyously from its spot of safety. "Thief! Thief!" a blue jay screamed. *Don't you dare intrude on my territory!* it seemed to say.

The harness jingled whenever the frisky horses snorted or tossed their heads. They seemed to be telling Andy, "We love plowing, too! We are enjoying this warm spring day every bit as much as you!"

With a dart, a robin winged through the woods before settling on a tree branch protruding out over the freshly plowed earth. He seemed to be asking, *Is it safe to look for worms or should I wait until the boy is farther down the field?* Andy laughed aloud at the bird. He loved supplying conversations for the birds and animals he observed.

Then he saw them. *The eagles!* Andy tipped his head back to watch as the two floated with the wind currents. They dipped and glided overhead as if to make sure he was doing a good job.

Wouldn't it be great to watch the eagles make a kill? Andy thought. But the eagles just kept floating, unaware of the plowing lad's wish. Their huge dark wings sparkled as the sunlight caught the glistening feathers with their white wing tips.

Reaching the end of the plowed land, Andy raised the plow. "Whoa!" he called, tugging on the reins. The horses stopped, their muscled shoulders showing a sheen of sweat. They needed no second command to take a breather before starting back down the field. Back and forth, back and forth, the horses plowed steadily all morning with a short rest after each round. Higher and higher the sun climbed until Andy decided it must be noon.

Yes, the sun is overhead! High time to take the horses in! I think they are as ready for lunch as I am! Unhitching the plow, Andy left it at the field's edge, ready to pick up where they left off plowing. He and the horses headed back toward the barn. As they came off the ridge onto the lane, the horses balked at an overhanging tree branch. *Now what?* Andy wondered as he tried to see what was keeping the horses from going under the thick branch that extended over the field lane. Suddenly, he saw a huge green-brown snake hanging from a higher branch above. Its tongue darted in and out as it hung motionless above the lane.

The sight unnerved him. *No wonder the horses were scared to go on!* Andy hurriedly turned the horses around and, tying them at the edge of the field, he took off running toward the barn. He didn't even stop to check if the snake had moved from the branch.

Grandpa's working at the gravel pit, so what should I do? He thought of his options as he ran and decided he should bike to the neighbors for help. Someone needed to kill the snake! He did not like guns; he could never kill the snake, but the neighbors were great hunters. They would love doing the job. Jumping on his bike, he raced down the road to Pete Jones' place.

"The men are all gone," Mrs. Jones told him. "But I can take you to get your grandfather. That snake definitely has to be shot!" She shuddered.

It didn't take long to drive to the nearby gravel pit. When Grandpa heard about the snake, he told his boss where he was going and returned with Mrs. Jones and his grandson.

"I haven't used my gun in years. It would be better to take one of yours," Grandpa suggested to Mrs. Jones. Their neighbor willingly agreed, stopping at her house for a gun. *Anything to get rid of the snake!* She shuddered again.

"I'll even drive you to your field lane," she offered in concern as she watched her stout elderly neighbor breathing heavily from the simple exertion of hurrying into her house to choose a gun.

"That would be good," Grandpa panted as he once again settled himself into the car while Andy swung onto his bicycle and peddled furiously ahead.

Andy was waiting for him at the field lane, and although Grandpa hurried as quickly as possible, it took some time to get back to the tree. When they got there, no snake could be seen anywhere. It had simply disappeared! Andy felt stupid for all the trouble he had caused for nothing. He kicked the dirt with the toe of his shoe. *Why hadn't he checked to see if the snake was still there after he had tied up the horses? Was he ever dumb!*

"No problem, son," Grandpa puffed, trying to make him feel better. "It's best to be safe. That must have been quite a snake! Would have liked to see it myself!"

I wish you could have, Andy thought, wishing the snake had remained on the branch. *There had been a snake! It scared the horses!* He felt sure it had been at least five feet long and five to six inches thick. It had hung down, staring at him with its beady little eyes as it flicked its tongue. Its greenish-brown skin had blended with the tree branches, but its flicking tongue had given it away. *Where had it come from? Where had it disappeared to?*

They never did see the snake again, though Andy watched for it each time he used the lane. When Grandpa explained that it was probably not a dangerous snake, Andy kept hoping it would show up again.

Three years after Mark King was ordained minister, he was ordained bishop. This time Andy was old enough to realize that because his father was now bishop of their church, some of his so-called friends would no longer want to associate with him. Being a minister's son had set him apart, and being a bishop's son would only intensify that rift. The other boys would never admit they were uncomfortable around him, but his relationship with the boys his age was somewhat strained. Many years would pass before Andy understood that this rift was not a curse, but a blessing. It helped him to make right choices and develop true friendships.

As Andy neared his sixteenth birthday, he wrestled with feelings of confusion and discouragement. Sixteen! It sounded both exciting and dreadful. He shrank back from the thought of attending singings and being with a large group of youth, yet at the same time he wished for time to move faster. *I don't even know what I want,* he found himself thinking. As he thought about the future, the issue of his adoption was never far from Andy's mind. *Does it bother my cousins that I am adopted? What will youth from the surrounding district churches hold against me more? Being adopted or being a bishop's son?*

Then one day Andy had a conversation with a taxi driver that hung heavily in his mind for a long time. It made him sick to his stomach, but no matter how hard he tried to erase the words, they continuously popped up to torment him.

"You folks hear about Fells' trial coming up?" their taxi driver asked. He was taking them to get their monthly supply of groceries at a large supermarket some distance from their home.

"No," Andy answered politely. This driver was not a familiar one. The neighbor who usually took them to buy groceries was recovering from a sprained ankle, and she had sent this man in her place.

"To make a long story short, Fells is a local teen about your age." The driver shot Andy a glance before continuing. "Been caught stealing and other things. I told my wife, 'What else can you expect? He was adopted!' "

Andy hoped his shock did not show. He could not answer. His stomach rolled and churned as sharp pain stabbed like needles, making him light-headed. His eyelid felt like it was out of control. He rolled the window partway down, taking in gulps of fresh air in an effort to dissipate the anguish he was feeling. *Adopted! Is that what people actually thought? Did they think adopted children weren't any good?*

"Not used to riding in a car?" the driver asked. "Getting carsick?"

"No," Fanny came to her son's rescue, not willing to say more to this prejudiced driver. Her anger simmered at his comments, but before they arrived at the market, she had made the choice to forgive him. He simply did not know better. It was easier for society to put the blame on something as simple as adoption than to accept responsibility for failing a child.

"What is the name of the young man you were talking about?" she asked the taxi driver before they got out of the car.

"Fells. Walter Fells. He is sixteen."

"I will pray for him; he must have never been taught the Bible way," Fanny told the man. He looked at her in amazement, then sat in thoughtful meditation long after Fanny and her son left to do their shopping.

"People don't understand adoption." Fanny said to Andy, as he glumly pushed the shopping cart for her, but she knew her words of comfort were not adequate. How could she help her son when cruel statements like this still pricked her like barbs? Strangers' remarks she could excuse, but when they came from family or church members?

Forgive. Yes, that was the only way. "Forgive again and again, seventy times seven," Mark had reminded her. She would have to have a talk with Andy, but first she would have to ask God to forgive her for hanging on to stinging barbs from the past.

Near this same time, as almost-sixteen-year-old Andy struggled again with the stigma evoked by adoption, his birth mother, Jan [O'Connor] Harding, lay in a hospital bed holding a newborn baby girl. More than fifteen and a half years had passed since her first baby had been born. Her teen years had been turbulent. Then, as an unwed mother, she had given birth to another son, Brent, five years ago. But in the last few years, Jan had settled down and gotten married. As she held her baby daughter, Jan thought of her first baby, the baby boy she never saw or held. Her heart throbbed with love for her tiny, very much alive baby daughter, softening the sense of aching loss that still came over her when she thought about the December morning more than fifteen years before when she left the hospital empty-handed. She had no idea that the son whom she believed was dead was now an Amish teenager, full of questions about her and about the past.

How she loved little Allison! This beautiful dark-haired baby girl belonged to her. No one was going to take her away. Sheer happiness flooded Jan as she thought of her husband counting the hours until he could take her and the baby home. He was bursting with pride and couldn't wait to show off his daughter to their friends.

January arrived, ushering in a new year and new experiences for Andy as he began attending young folks' activities. He had attended these activities for only several months when a group of youth who refused to join in the singing singled him out. "Come on," they urged, "join us next Saturday evening for some fun!"

In this heavily populated Amish area, several church districts made up the large local youth group. Within this large group of youth were two distinct groups. One was called the "singing youth." They actually participated in the singings held at the house of the family who hosted church that day. These youth were serious about their Christian lives and had either joined church or were planning to do so while they were still young. The other group was referred to as the "fast youth" or "car youth." They owned cars or associated with friends who owned cars. Their primary interest in life was to have fun while they had the chance. Most of them said they planned to join church someday, but not until they were ready to settle down and get married.

Andy did not fit in with the car youth at all. When he continually refused to go with them, they ignored him. Who wanted to be friends with the bishop's son who acted so righteous? Not they! Andy had not joined church, but skipping the singings was out of the question for him.

There were times when Andy had doubts. Maybe if he joined with the car youth, he would actually have closer friends. *What would it be like to be popular like Phil?* he wondered as he stood along a barn wall one evening watching as other youth vied for Phil's attention. *Was Phil as carefree as he acted or was it a cover-up?* Somehow, the knowledge of his parents' disapproval and fear of rejection from the fast youth kept Andy away from them and proved to be a safeguard in his teen years.

"Choose what is right in God's sight," his parents

had encouraged Andy when he joined the youth group. Whenever he thought of them, a warm feeling wrapped around his heart. He loved his dear parents. He knew they prayed for him, and that knowledge sustained him, giving him courage to stand for what was right.

One Sunday evening, Andy decided to leave the singing before it was over. Corn harvest was in full swing, and tomorrow would be another long day. As he rounded the corner of the barn, he heard Omar and Nelson deep in conversation. Not wanting to interrupt them he stopped, ready to go the other way, when Omar said, "Imagine! The church is finally allowing old bachelor Jeremiah to get married!" Both boys roared with laughter as though it were the biggest joke of the evening.

Andy slipped further into the shadows. He could not possibly let the two boys catch him listening! He knew Jeremiah Miller. Adopted Jeremiah Miller. Friendly, kind Jeremiah Miller. Twenty-nine-year-old Jeremiah Miller was a close neighbor, but he was from a stricter church district. Andy's gut clenched. He would ask his mom. She would know what the boys were talking about.

"Yes, Andy." His mom sighed as she faced her tall son across the table. "I know what Omar and Nelson were discussing. It is not an easy story to tell, but it's better if you hear it from me than from someone else." She paused, praying that what she had to say would not fuel the feelings of rejection her son struggled with.

"We all know Jeremiah was adopted as a young boy. Dad has a high respect for him and his parents. I have firsthand knowledge of what happened because his mother first came to me six years ago for advice. We share a common bond, the bond of motherhood through adoption, and that has developed into a friendship.

"Jeremiah is in an unfortunate church situation. Because his birth mother was a victim of sexual assault, the church will not allow any of their girls to date Jeremiah. Andy, that is not Biblical at all." She reached across the table to touch his ice-cold hand.

Fanny saw the look in her son's eyes and the telltale jumping of his eyelid that told her he was in distress. "I can see the questions in your eyes, Andy," she said. "Listen to me, son. I believe you've been bothered by some of these things for quite a few years. I wish I had addressed them with you when you were in public school. Did your classmates suggest that your situation was the same as Jeremiah's?"

"Yes," came Andy's tortured whisper, piercing his mother's heart. "They always said that I was one of 'those' children."

"Son," Fanny spoke in a quiet, intense voice. "Truthfully, we don't know who your birth mother was, or in what circumstances she conceived and gave birth to you. But this is what we do know. Every baby is precious in God's sight. Every person is born with a sinful nature that needs to be washed clean in the blood of Jesus Christ. The Bible tells us God is no respecter of persons. Everyone, Andy, no matter what his origin, is covered and cared for by God before he is born."

Andy nodded, his head bowed. "Years ago Grandpa told me the same thing." His voice cracked, and it took effort to talk. It felt as if he had to tear each word away from the heaviness he bore in his heart. Did he fall in the same category as Jeremiah? Knowing God was no respecter of persons did not bring relief, as the rift he felt between himself and his fellow youth seemed to be a widening chasm.

When his mom made no comment, he looked up to see her wiping tears from her eyes. Seeing her tears brought comfort. Mom *did* know his pain. Suddenly, he found his voice.

"Are you talking about the verse found in Psalm 139?" he asked. "Is it the one that says 'thou hast covered me in my mother's womb'?"

Startled by his question, Fanny nodded. "So you know that verse? I'm glad you do! It is a good one to remember."

"Grandpa told me to look up the verse when I was only eight or so. I have never forgotten it," Andy explained. "Maybe he guessed that I was having a hard time at school. We went out to the woods to find the eagles' nest, and while we were talking, he told me about that verse. When I came home I told Dad, and he found it for me."

Fanny smiled through her tears, silently thanking God for sending others to help her son when she didn't even know he needed help. She took a deep breath and plunged ahead. She still had to finish Jeremiah's story.

"Son," she said. "It is only natural that you wonder about your mother and the circumstances of your birth. That is OK. I wonder about it too. Always remember though, that God knows all about you and we must let the unknown rest with Him."

"Thanks, Mom, I try to do that, but the question is always there. Who will want me if I'm actually like Jeremiah, one of 'those children'? Maybe everyone already thinks that but is too polite to say it in my hearing. Maybe I should try to find out who my birth mother is. But if I don't, I can make up fantastic stories of both of my parents being killed or some other scenario where I'm taken to the local hospital to wait until a lonely, childless, Amish couple adopts me."

Fanny's heart throbbed painfully as she heard her son express the haunting questions he lived with. *Did he not know that she and Mark loved him like their own flesh and blood? Did their son not feel the security and safety they had tried to provide for him as a child and now as a young adult? Did he not feel their prayers surrounding him, covering him, drawing him to the Father in heaven?* She pushed her own pain away as she focused on her son's need and continued.

"Those are real questions, Andy, and I'm glad you are sharing your feelings with me. Let me finish telling you about Jeremiah. Last week his mother told me that Jeremiah has been working in another district for a man who has a widowed daughter. The daughter and Jeremiah have gotten to know each other and want to be married. The girl's parents respect Jeremiah and are not opposed to their marriage, but once more Jeremiah's church was against it. This time the girl's church disagreed with Jeremiah's church's decision. They feel there is nothing to keep the two from marrying. Finally Jeremiah's church consented to let him marry and let him keep his church membership."

"Thanks, Mom, for telling me and for encouraging me. I don't know why I struggle with this when I have the best parents a fellow could want. I guess I need to trust more and not worry so much, but that seems impossible." Andy scratched his head as he rose from the table. "I'm glad for

Jeremiah. I'm glad her church stepped in, but I just don't understand why Omar and Nelson laughed like they did."

"Neither do I, but it's best not to dwell on negative things."

Thankfulness filled Andy's heart as he went to his room. *Where would I be without my parents?*

The next morning, grabbing a jacket off the hook by the door, Andy hopped on his bike to ride to his grandparents' farm. Crisp fall air told of winter's coming. The morning sun hung like a brilliant ball in the cloudless blue dome overhead. *A perfect day to pick corn and watch the eagles soaring,* he thought as he leaned forward over the handlebars, peddling furiously to gain momentum for the long hill ahead.

Oh, to be able to farm for a living! Andy had never given up this boyhood dream. It seemed every year the longing intensified instead of lessening as he thought it should. How could his dream ever materialize when his dad was a day laborer? *How long will it be until I, too, will need to work at an hourly job?* Andy groaned at the thought of being shut up in a shop all day or hammering nails day in and day out.

I'm surprised Dad still lets me work at the farm, but that will change once I have my eighteenth birthday. Only boys who grow up on farms seem to be able to continue farming when they strike out on their own. At least I'll be able to come on Saturdays and after work, Andy consoled himself.

When noon came, Andy ate his lunch and then left the horses resting while he hiked back to his favorite spot to view the eagles' oak tree. This time he was privileged to see the mother eagle bringing food to her young.

Andy sat motionless as he watched, moved by the eagle's care for her babies. Hope rose within him. *If God is so well able to provide for baby eagles, couldn't He provide for him as well? If only he could know more about God!* Bowing his head, Andy prayed a prayer that came from the depths of his soul.

"God, show me how to find you and know who you are."

Fire!

1984

*F*ussing again! What satisfaction do my brothers get out of quarrelling with each other? It's beyond me. Andy sighed as he sat down in the semi-darkness on their top basement step and pulled off his muddy boots. Rainy days always left this old part of their house feeling dark and dreary. He entered the dim downstairs kitchen where his brothers squabbled over the dishes they were washing. He lit the floor lamp standing by the kitchen table.

"See if you can work without fighting," he encouraged, but Joshua stuck out his tongue and made a face, not at all happy to have big brother's interference.

"Where's Dad?" Andy asked, ignoring the protruding tongue.

"In the shop," Joshua answered, handing a knife back to his brother before demanding, "Wash your dishes clean! Can't you do better than that?"

Andy sighed again, left the kitchen, and headed back up the steps. Several years ago they had added to their basement home, and now the bedrooms and living room were upstairs while the kitchen was still in the basement.

Andy had just put his boots back on when he heard a loud noise. *Boom!*

Those boys! Now what? he thought as he stopped with his hand on the outside door handle.

"What's that?" Mom poked her head out of their bedroom door.

"Just the boys, I'll go down and settle them," Andy offered.

Fanny untied the strings of her dirty apron. "Thanks, Andy. Dad wants to go visit Ed Miller's family since their little girl Susanna just spent a week in the hospital. I need to be ready to leave when he gets back from harnessing the horse."

As Andy headed downstairs, he smelled smoke. "What's happening?" he yelled as he raced for the kitchen.

Andy's shout brought Mom running downstairs behind him. Thick smoke met them at the kitchen entrance. The top of the lamp lay undetected in the corner of the doorway. All they saw were crackling flames sweeping across the ceiling, eating into the tinder-dry ceiling boards, and spewing out a cloud of blackness in their wake.

Andy grabbed the fire extinguisher beside the door and began dousing the spreading ceiling fire. "Where are the boys?" Mom cried in panic. Running out of the house, she ran screaming down the lane, "Fire! Fire!"

Her stocking feet plunged through water puddles and mud. Her apron flapped around with its untied strings floating behind. Neighbors across the road heard her cries and ran over to help. But by the time Dad arrived from the shop and Mom had returned with the neighbors, Andy had put out the fire. Two frightened young boys appeared from around the corner of the house, wondering if it was safe to enter.

Joshua had had the presence of mind to have Joseph escape with him through a basement window in the pantry off the kitchen. When the lamp had exploded, it had landed in a smoldering heap beside the kitchen door, and they had been too afraid to go past it.

What a black, smoky mess the fire had made! Neighbors helped wash off the walls, ceiling, furniture, and the cupboards and their contents. Thankfully, Joshua had shut the pantry door behind him when he and Joseph opened the window and crawled through. This kept smoke out of the pantry and saved them a lot of work.

"I think I figured out what happened," their neighbor said as he studied the pieces of the blown lamp. "This lamp is fairly old, right?"

"Yes," Mark answered. "We've had it since we were married."

"My thinking is that with age the tank must have developed a defect. I imagine that gas escaped and made contact with the heat from the burning lamp, which caused the explosion." He looked up at the large patch of burned ceiling. "Several more minutes and I doubt if the house would still be here." Everyone was silent as they digested his sobering words.

Andy kept seeing the flames racing across the kitchen ceiling. *God certainly kept us from serious harm. Maybe from losing the whole house, but definitely from losing my two brothers.* He shuddered to think what could have happened if the blown lamp had flown in the other direction, right where Joshua and Joseph were doing dishes.

Would one or both brothers be in the hospital, badly burned?
What if I had already left the house? Or worst yet, what if the
lamp had blown when I was standing at that exact spot mo-
ments earlier? I could have been knocked out; the fire could
have gotten away . . . Would I have been ready to face God?
Andy's mind churned with questions he longed to have answered. It seemed all his life he had had unanswered questions burning within.

Suddenly phrases from a verse that he had heard his Dad
quote several times started running through his mind. It
was about eagles. Phrases about waiting upon the Lord and
mounting up on wings like eagles kept repeating themselves in his head. He knew he had read the verse before. It
seemed like it was in Isaiah, maybe chapter 40. Andy had
to know what the whole verse said. It seemed so unusual for words of the verse to keep going around in his head
like that. He went and found the Bible. Scanning through
Isaiah 40, at last his eyes landed on verse 31, "But they that
wait upon the Lord shall renew their strength; they shall
mount up with wings as eagles, they shall run, and not be
weary; and they shall walk, and not faint."

Waiting on the Lord. What did that mean? To have the
strength of an eagle would certainly be a good thing. To
soar on wings above the treetops with glistening sunlight
warming your back, to see low-lying mist blanketing the
morning hills, to glide over rushing streams . . . It would
be nice to be that strong!

"Not physical, but spiritual strength," Andy spoke out
loud to himself as he prepared for bed. "And I am in sore
need of some. This heaviness I feel makes me feel very weak!"

"Lord," he prayed. "What does it mean to wait on you? I believe the Bible. I trust in you, but I don't know why I can't get rid of this heaviness in my heart."

Andy stood at the door of his brothers' bedroom watching them stretched out in sleep. How he loved those exasperating younger brothers! He was so grateful that God had kept them safe. He wanted to be a good example for them to follow, but he felt so confused right now. One thing was certain. He needed to have a talk with his dad. Soon!

Moving Plans 11

1984

"Well, boys," Dad announced, scraping the last bit of pot roast from his plate, "I smell an apple pie cooling somewhere, but I believe we should help Mom clear the table and do dishes before she serves it. Then Mom and I want to discuss something with you while we eat our pie."

"Yes! Andy can wash the dishes!" Joseph said triumphantly. Everyone laughed at his eagerness.

"That I will," Andy offered as he picked up his dishes and headed for the sink. "But I'll warn you; I'm a fast washer!"

The younger boys scrambled to find dish towels. They were determined to dry dishes as fast as Andy washed them.

"I didn't know you could wash dishes so fast," Joseph's towel flew around and around the plate he was drying. He and Joshua were having a hard time keeping the drainer empty. "I didn't even know you knew how to wash dishes," he admitted, reaching for a bowl before it settled completely into the drainer.

"Who do you think washed dishes all those years before you and Joshua could do them?" Andy stopped washing and looked directly at his younger brothers. Seeing their faces, it dawned on him. They were serious. They honestly thought he had never washed dishes.

"Well, boys, I remember Mom saying I stood by this sink almost every day of my life once I was old enough to use that high stool you see by the wall over there." Both boys' eyes widened at the tall green stool they sometimes used as an extra chair. *Andy must have been really little!* He could imagine that thought spinning in both their minds as they pictured how short he must have been to have had to stand on a stool that tall to reach the sink. Andy kept his grin to himself. This was too much fun to spoil things now.

"Once I got too tall for that stool, Mom let me graduate to the lower one she uses to get the dishes from the top cupboards." His brother's glance swung over to the stool they were all too familiar with. It didn't seem like very long ago they had stood on the same stool toiling over mounds of dirty dishes. Had Andy actually done dishes all those years? He certainly could wash dishes fast.

Dad brought the last of the dishes from the kitchen table and stayed to listen.

"Andy! You couldn't have washed dishes from the green stool! You are just making it up!" Joshua retorted.

Dad laughed. "He used the green stool all right, and it was at the sink, but not to wash dishes. Mom could never fill the sink with water without little Andy dragging over the stool and begging to help. His help was splashing in the water, making a mess!"

"Dad's right! But I did wash an awful lot of dishes in my growing up years," Andy said as he swished his dishrag around in the water gurgling out the drain. "So now you know why I can wash so fast? Remember I'm five years older than you, Joshua, and I had no brothers to help."

Andy glanced at Dad, who winked at the younger boys.

Joseph just grinned, then blurted, "That was fun!"

"It was!" Andy smiled.

Warm apple pie drew the family back to the table where Mom was dishing it out. Everyone waited expectantly for Dad to begin.

"How would you boys feel about moving to Grandpa Yoder's farm?" he asked.

Andy's fork stopped in mid-air. *The farm? Had he heard right?*

"Grandpa is finding it harder and harder to keep up with the demands of farm work," Dad continued. "Since Andy is doing the bulk of the work anyway, they wondered if we would want to move to the farm so that Andy could take over the work there."

Move to the farm? Andy had no reservations at all. He had always dreamed of living on a farm. His mind whirled with the possibilities. When he caught the words, "work of building a Dawdy house," he realized he had missed some of what was said.

"Where will Grandpas build?" Joshua asked, sparing Andy the need to have Dad repeat what he had missed.

"You know where the curve in the lane is? Where the ground slopes up to meet the ridge on the right hand side? Once the grass slope is leveled, there will be just enough space to build a small house."

Andy pictured a little house at the curve and liked what he saw. It would be close to the big house, yet the two houses would be far enough apart for both families to feel like they had their own property.

"Looks like Andy might not be sold on the idea. He hasn't said a word!" Dad's tone dripped with disappointment, but there was a knowing twinkle in his eye.

"Sorry, Dad," Andy answered sheepishly. "I was already picturing Grandpa's house and all the possibilities living on the farm presented."

"I knew it, son! Just teasing you.

"Uncle Jonas needs a new hired man on his farm, and he asked if you would consider working for him part-time too. Grandpa also suggested we work toward starting to milk cows again on his farm. We would probably do that kind of slowly, taking three to four years to build up a herd. By that time Uncle Jonas's boys should be old enough to help their dad, and you would no longer be needed there.

"So, what do you think, Andy? Is farming what you want to do?"

"Yes, farming has been my dream," Andy replied. "For sure, you couldn't give me a better job! I would like to work for Uncle Jonas, and with them living on the next farm that should work out well."

"Mom and I are glad this opportunity is here for you." Dad looked at his younger sons. "Are you boys ready to learn farming, too?" he asked.

Joshua wasn't so sure. "Would I really have to milk cows? I'd rather work in Harry's wood shop when I am old enough."

"We shall see," said Dad. "You might decide that milking cows is the best job around!"

Work began on the Dawdy house, and Andy moved in with Grandpas while it was being built. Now that he was responsible for more of the work on the farm, Andy found his days full and challenging. Helping Uncle Jonas, keeping up with field work, and getting the barn ready for milk cows left Andy with little time to think of anything else.

One day after both his parents and grandparents had moved into their new homes, Andy paused in his work to watch the eagles soaring overhead. Seeing them brought back memories of the day of the fire, the day when he had read Isaiah 40:31 and wondered what it meant for him. He still had the same questions he had had then, questions he needed answers for. *I need to talk to Dad*, he thought again.

The piercing cry of the male eagle echoed across the field where Andy was planting corn. "Surely, God created you, king of the air," he whispered in breathless wonder. *And God sees me, a mere speck, and knows all about me. It seems like my restlessness has faded a bit. Or am I just too busy to think? Is this part of waiting on God? I know I need to make a decision about joining church. Classes start in six weeks. If I don't decide soon, I'll need to wait until next summer.*

Before that week was over, before Andy had found time to talk with his dad, the community was shocked to learn of a tragic accident that claimed the lives of two teen boys from another church district.

Andy was deep in thought as he followed the two caskets to the cemetery. *What if I were one of the ones in a casket?* He shrank back at the thought of dying. Snatches of words and verses from both sermons were branded in his mind. "He that heareth my word, and believeth . . . shall not come into condemnation."[1] The minister had said, "Condemnation refers to eternal death." *Did the two boys who died have the assurance that they would not face eternal death?* Andy's eyelid twitched, his hands felt clammy, and his heart raced. *If the minister would ask me, what would I answer? I believe in God, but He seems far away.* A deep sigh escaped as Andy contemplated the question.

What had the second minister said? Something about the hope he had for each person listening, the hope of salvation, and the promise God gives to each individual who overcomes. The minister had then recited Revelation 21:7. " 'He that overcometh shall inherit all things; and I will be his God, and he shall be my son.' " *That's what I want!* Andy's heart cried as he drew in a deep breath.

As he headed home, Andy was glad to be alone and have time to sort out his troubling thoughts. With the gentle, steady trotting of his horse, he felt a calmness stealing over him. *Tonight I am going to talk to Dad,* he determined. *I dare not put it off any longer.*

"Dad," Andy said that evening when the two were alone, "how do I know God as I should? What does it mean to wait on the Lord? I have this longing to know Him, but how do I do that?" His left eyelid revealed his inner agitation.

"Andy, Mom and I have been praying for you. We sensed you were struggling to know God's purpose for your life. The longing you have to know God is simply God speaking to you. He, too, longs for you to know Him. A father loves his children and longs to have a close relationship with them. The same is true with God. As your mind has

---

[1] John 5:24

developed and matured, God has drawn you to Himself, longing to develop a personal relationship with you.

"This relationship means accepting God as Lord of your life. It will mean giving up your will, or desires, to do whatever God commands. Man is born with the tendency to sin, and God is the only one who can cleanse our sins. It was Jesus' death on the cross that makes it possible for us to have a relationship with God. The death and resurrection of Jesus have made it possible for us to approach God."

Andy nodded, then blurted in frustration, "So I just say I will join church, and what God wants of me will be clear?"

"You know the familiar Scriptures, 'all have sinned'[2] and 'if thou shalt confess with thy mouth the Lord Jesus, and believe in thine heart that God hath raised him from the dead, thou shalt be saved.'[3] To know God, we first must confess. Belief follows. We don't stop there, but, by obedience, we continue to grow and learn."

Andy nodded again as light dawned. "I must first confess my sinfulness and then believe that God has saved me. It seems too simple. It feels like I need to do more, but maybe that thought comes from Satan."

"It does, son. We can never earn our salvation. Salvation comes only when we confess and believe and live in faithful obedience to God's Word and the church."

"Thanks, Dad, I do understand. Now can you explain what this verse means? 'They that wait upon the LORD shall renew their strength'[4]? What does it mean to wait on the Lord?"

---

[2] Romans 3:23
[3] Romans 10:9
[4] Isaiah 40:31

"The eagle verse," Dad smiled. "Mom told me that you like that verse too. God's strength and power are likened to that of an eagle. Even the strongest of people get tired at times—weary of pressures, of resisting temptation, even weary of doing what is right when it would be easier to join the crowd. God never gets tired. Never! He never wearies of us coming to Him for help. When you feel as if life is crushing you and you can't go another step, remember, God never grows tired. We can call on Him for help, for direction, and for strength to endure anything that confronts us, and then all we must do is wait, with the faith that He will answer and come through for us. God will renew our strength, and we will be able to run, to live the Christian life without fainting or giving up."

"I should have talked to you sooner. I would have saved myself a lot of frustration." Andy rubbed his left eye. He could feel the lid fluttering. "Pray for me, Dad. I want to join church this summer, but I don't feel good enough, and I worry that others also think that about me. But you've helped me see that I must stop dwelling on my feelings and trust God completely for everything. I have so little faith, but I want more."

"Bring all your troubled thoughts to God," Dad said. "And remember, the Bible says, 'Faith cometh by hearing, and hearing by the word of God.'[5] Mom and I are definitely praying for you."

---

[5] Romans 10:17

Waiting on God

12

1984

Eight young people stood and filed out of the room behind the bishop and ministers to attend their first instruction class. Seven more classes would follow, to prepare the new applicants for baptism. These classes would be held on Sundays at the beginning of the church services while the rest of the congregation sang.

Andy was thrilled that so many other young people were making this decision too. The funerals of the two youth had been sobering. He was especially thankful that Sam and Caleb had joined instruction class. They had been running with the car youth since turning sixteen.

His left eyelid gave an involuntary jump when he spied quiet Sarah Raber. Two other girls from the east district were there too. He had forgotten that some from the east district had asked to take instruction classes under their church district since they had no acting bishop this summer. Andy was doubly glad he had made the decision to join church this season. Sarah had attracted his attention for some time, and if she, too, would be joining church . . . He pushed the thought from his mind and turned his full attention to what was taking place. *You didn't join for that reason,* he chided himself.

"Do you voluntarily consent to be counseled to join the church?" his dad asked each young person. After each expressed the desire to do so, he explained, "At each instruction class we will study one of the seven ordinances. They are communion, feet washing, the head veiling, anointing with oil, marriage, the holy kiss, and baptism. The final class will be held Friday evening before baptism when we will conclude with the Articles of Faith."

As the instruction classes progressed, Andy was both challenged and drawn by Sarah Raber's personality. *She might be small in stature, but she certainly possesses a mighty inner strength! Will I ever have the courage to ask her for a date? If I do, will the fact that I'm adopted make a difference in her answer?*

At the sixth instruction class, Andy's father asked each of the applicants, "Are you willing to submit to the teachings of the church? Now is the time to determine what your answer will be." The room became deathly quiet. This was a crucial decision. Andy remembered times past when one or two youth came out of the room with head down and left the church service. Those youth had found Christian discipleship too constricting. The allure of the world drew them like a magnet. Instead of denying self and taking up the cross of Jesus Christ, they had turned their backs on the peace and joy Jesus offered, choosing instead the deceit of worldly pleasures. With grieving hearts, the church had prayed for these youth, longing for them to find their way back to holy, righteous living.

Andy's heart beat rapidly as he and all the youth present gave affirmative answers. He noticed that his dad's eyes glistened with tears. An overwhelming love for his father washed over Andy as Mark said, "God bless each of you as you endeavor to walk in faithfulness with our Lord and Saviour Jesus Christ."

Mark took out his handkerchief, and wiping his eyes, he looked into the expectant faces sitting before him. His shepherd heart rejoiced. Eight souls had chosen to be baptized and become a part of the church; eight young men and women were looking to him, a mortal man with many failings, to direct them spiritually. *Lord, this task is too great for me! Lead me each step,* Mark's soul cried out to God for divine wisdom.

Aloud he said, "I'm going to read parts of a prayer called, 'A Prayer of Devout Parents for Their Children.' You know I am the parent to only one of you, yet as bishop of our church, God has given me a parental position in looking out for your spiritual instruction. I'm sure most of you have heard this prayer in your own homes. Listen carefully. Today I am praying it as my prayer and as a challenge for each one of you. I have replaced several words so the prayer will be personal.

" 'O Lord! Dear, faithful God and Father, Creator, and Sustainer of all living beings! Grant to [each youth] also thy grace: that [I] may [instruct these youth] in the discipline and admonition of the Lord, and in all righteousness, and that [I] may lead them in the fear of God and in virtue.

" 'Let them not fall into wickedness, nor be an offense to others. Be their protection in every [spiritual] danger lest they perish suddenly . . .' "[1]

---

[1] Taken from *In Meiner Jugend,* a devotional reader in German and English.

At the eighth service, a vote was taken by the church to see if all were agreed to let the applicants be baptized. When an affirmative vote was taken and the announcement given that the baptismal service would be in two weeks, the instruction class was told, "You will meet at Mark King's place at 6:30 the Friday evening prior to baptism for your last class on the Articles of Faith."

Two days later Andy finished choring just as the morning sunrise broke over the peaceful farmland, banishing the last tinges of darkness and low-lying mists. Cows were being turned out to pasture, and hungry men and chore boys kicked off their barn boots, their mouths watering at the tantalizing kitchen smells wafting out the open windows of various farmhouses. Andy took his usual seat on the bench along the back of the table, bowed his head in silent prayer with the rest of the family, and then began eating. Morning conversation was always minimal until breakfast was eaten and Dad again bowed his head for silent prayer.

"So what do you hope to do today, Andy?" Mom wondered.

"I'm hoping to finish cutting our hay before going over to help Uncle Jonas put his in the barn," Andy answered. "This week will be a busy one!"

But Andy had no idea that his plans were about to be completely changed. God had arranged a divine appointment. Before Andy even arrived at the hayfield, Grandpa Yoder died at home from a massive heart attack.

Grandpa's passing left Andy numb with grief. Grandpa gone? He wasn't ready to give up his grandfather. Yet,

Grandpa's death and funeral just before his baptism made Andy more seriously consider the choice he was making. He felt a deep desire to live a committed life of faithfulness. His hope was heaven, and he wanted to live in a way that was acceptable to God and the church. Heaven seemed closer, daily life lost its attractive hold on him, and Andy's grief found solace in the knowledge that if he walked faithfully with God and the church, he would one day see his grandfather again.

The Sunday morning of Andy's baptism dawned clear and cloudless. As Andy left the barn after harnessing his horse, he found himself looking heavenward, once more wishing his grandfather would be here to share in his baptism, wishing for another chance to talk to him. "Grandpa," his heart whispered, "I never thanked you for all you taught me. I wish I had. Today is very important to me; my heart is so full I can't explain the emotions I am feeling, but I know you would understand when I say that today I am completing my adoption. I know you would tell me it is the best decision I have made, and I agree." Andy smiled self-consciously as he carried on his one-sided conversation. Though the pain of Grandfather's death caused an ache that would not leave, he also felt inner peace and joy that God would now call him a son.

I have never forgotten the day Grandpa told me that God knew about me before I was even born. I wonder how often I reread that verse or thought of it and received courage because God cared for me before I was born! And now, my baptism today is an outward sign showing my inner change, my desire to live a holy life. I am probably the only youth in our class thinking that today is the completion of my adoption into the family of God! But that's all right; I'm just glad I can claim that adoption.

Andy paused outside the house door. "Lord God," his heart cried out in silent prayer. "Thank you for giving me my parents. Thank you for placing me in this Amish home. I have been raised in a safe place. I love the verse that says, 'Behold, what manner of love the Father hath bestowed upon us, that we should be called the sons of God.'[2] Thank you, Lord, for your love. Thank you for accepting me as a son. In your eyes I am no different from the other youth taking the same vows." Andy opened the door into the house. He had better eat breakfast quickly. He didn't want to be late for his baptism.

Peace flooded Andy's soul as he answered *yes* to the four baptismal vows:

Can you confess, "I believe that Jesus Christ is the Son of God"?

Do you also confess this to be a Christian doctrine, church, and brotherhood to which you are about to submit?

Do you denounce the world, the devil and all his doings, as well as your own flesh and blood, and desire to serve only Jesus Christ, who died on the cross for you?

Do you also promise, in the presence of God and His church, with the Lord's help to support these doctrines and regulations, to earnestly fill your place in the church, to help counsel and labor, and not depart from the same, come what may, life or death?

Reverential awe washed over Andy as he knelt and

---

[2] 1 John 3:1

received water baptism. Joy such as he had never known left him feeling like he was floating on wings like the eagles, soaring above all earthly cares.

"Thank you, Lord God. I want to be a faithful son." Andy's heart cry of praise rose above the building's roof. It wafted heavenward, bringing glory to the Creator of heaven and earth. Andy's desire to know God was being fulfilled.

Changes

13

1985

Andy's nineteenth birthday came and went before he got up enough courage to ask Sarah Raber for a date. At last he steeled his nerves, asked the weighty question, and thrilled with joy when she answered *yes.*

Sarah accepted! He wanted to shout out to anyone who would listen. *I am walking on the clouds!* The new tree leaves took on a brighter, greener sheen. The horses worked harder. His small herd of milk cows gave abundant milk. But now the eagles overhead didn't appear quite as majestic as usual. A petite, dark-haired lady held a keener attraction than his long-admired outdoor friends.

Several months and several dates later, Andy was shocked when Roy, one of the youth boys from Sarah's district, stopped in on a Saturday evening and causally mentioned that Sarah had spent all day with Leroy and a group of his friends on a canoe trip the day before. *How could she?* Andy agonized after Roy had left. He felt as if his whole life was crashing down around him. *Doesn't Sarah realize she is the only girl who interests me? Can't she tell how much I enjoy each evening I am with her?*

Why would she spend a whole day with Leroy, when he is not her type? Or don't I know Sarah like I think I do? Andy's numb mind tried to make sense of what he had heard. He tried to think about their last date. Had he detected any aloofness in Sarah? Had she been different than on previous dates? Andy's mind didn't want to function; the heavy, devastating weight within brought forth a groan.

"Lord God," he cried. "Show me what you have for my life. I was so sure of Sarah. Let there be a mistake somewhere. If not, help me to accept it." His short prayer brought no relief, but it did help him to think more clearly.

Sarah had seemed ready and willing each time he asked her if he could take her home again. *Sarah is the one person I find easy to talk to! Why haven't I ever asked if she knew I was adopted? Did she find out? Is that why she went with Leroy on the canoe outing? Maybe I was wrong not to mention my background. It's not that I didn't consider asking her if she knew I was adopted. It was simply too hard to broach the subject!*

Andy's mind tried to reason everything out. He had felt like he wanted to know Sarah a little better before discussing his background, but according to Amish custom they still hadn't had enough dates for him to ask her if she wanted to go steady.[1] He had planned to ask her if she knew about his adoption then. *Now what?* He kicked an offending stone in his path, sending it spinning across the barn lot. *Have I lost my chance? For sure, I am not attending the youth activity this coming Sunday evening!*

When Andy didn't show up that Sunday evening, Sarah wondered where he was. *Probably sick,* she surmised, disappointed. *I certainly will miss him asking if I want a way home tonight. He is the finest boy in the group!* She felt blessed that he had noticed her, but she wondered if he felt the same way she did. *If two people know they want to date only each*

---

[1] This term is used in Amish circles to indicate regular dating.

other, why do they have to wait at least three months until they go steady? She sighed. *I wish I had just stayed home tonight!*

"Hey, Sarah," her cousin Aaron J. called, motioning to her when the singing was over. She followed him out the door and around the corner of the house. "Hey, you looking for a ride home tonight?" he asked.

"What do you mean? Andy's not here, is he?" She gave herself away with her quick answer.

Aaron J. looked queerly at her. "You waiting on Andy?"

"He must be sick or something because I didn't see him come in tonight, but yes, if my nosey cousin needs to know, I was waiting on him," she retorted. "But don't you dare tell him! I don't know what he thinks of me."

"Believe me! If Andy has taken you home even just once, you don't need to worry about what he thinks of you!" Her cousin's statement sent happy circles dancing around her heart.

"If Andy isn't here, why would I be looking for a way home?" she suddenly asked, her mouth pursed at his odd question.

Aaron J. cleared his throat. "Don't be mad at me, but Leroy said there was something going between you and him, and I should see if you needed a way home."

Sarah's anger flared. "Who did he tell that to?" she demanded.

"Well," Aaron J. stalled, "I guess everyone but you," he finally admitted.

"Aaron J.! Is that why Andy isn't here tonight? Did Leroy tell you that when I was asked to go on the canoe trip, I had no idea he was along or that I would be thrown with him all day? Or that I was invited as his date without my knowing anything about it? Did he?"

"No, he sure didn't," said Aaron J. "And yes, that probably is the reason Andy's not here," he said. He decided not to tell Sarah what Roy had told him, how that when he'd told Andy about Sarah spending the day with Leroy, Roy had feared that Andy would pass out. Andy's face had turned a pasty white, but he only stared ahead, not asking any questions or saying a word until Roy had left.

Tears spilled out of Sarah's eyes at the thought of Andy at home, thinking she had rejected him for immature, self-centered, girl-crazy Leroy. Leroy had pestered her before, but up until the day of the canoe outing, she had basically been able to ignore him. "Aaron J., take me home right now," Sarah sniffed. "Please! What must Andy be thinking?"

"I'll make sure he hears the right version of the story." Aaron J. tried to comfort his distraught cousin. "Don't worry your pretty little head. Andy isn't one to hold grudges."

"Thanks, cousin, I feel a little better. I may as well be honest with you. The way I feel now, if Andy never asks me again, I will be an old maid the rest of my life!"

"Whoa, that is a strong statement! Andy is one lucky fellow." The two cousins shared a laugh as Aaron J. drove into Sarah's lane.

Aaron J. kept his word, and Andy did hear the correct version of what had happened. Joy filled his heart, but he also felt a twinge of shame for letting the incident shake him so deeply. "I was wrong to let the rumor weaken my trust in God and destroy everything I believed about Sarah. I should have been man enough to ask her myself," he told his mother as he shared with her what had happened. "Rejection always puts me flat on my back. Poor Sarah, if she will have me, I'd better grow up!"

Andy wasted no time in opening his heart to Sarah when they left the next singing together. "We haven't dated three months yet, but I need to know how you feel about dating someone who's adopted. I should have talked to you about this the first time I asked you, but I guess I was too chicken," Andy confessed.

"Being adopted makes no difference to me," Sarah quickly assured him. "Your character and standing with the church is what I'm concerned about. I feel blessed that you have been asking to take me home," she finished, giving him a shy smile.

Sarah did not live in Andy's church district. He had a forty-five minute drive to her house by horse and buggy. Every other Saturday night was recognized as date night for couples going steady. Andy would spend the night at Sarah's house, bunking with her younger brother. The next morning, he took her to church. After staying for the Sunday evening singing, he took Sarah home, leaving her house at midnight for the long drive home.

It was almost a year since Andy and Sarah had been going steady. "Sarah, aren't we thankful?" Andy asked one evening, leaving the question hanging. Sarah knew what he was referring to.

"Yes, very," Sarah agreed, "but my heart weeps for Phil and Mary Anna. The shame of having to get married is big, but becoming parents in five months! That would be overwhelming. She is just seventeen."

"I am grateful they confessed and want to join church," Andy said.

"Yes," Sarah agreed. Both grew quiet, lost in thoughts pertaining to the confession they had witnessed that morning.

"It would be hard to have no wedding festivity, no time to prepare, only the harsh reality of the consequences of sin. But God forgives, and we must, too." Andy finally broke the silence. "We will need to pray for them. The reaping of sin is never easy.

"Hearing what we did today brings back some of my biggest childhood fears," Andy continued. "I will confess, Sarah, the fear that my birth parents weren't married and the fear that perhaps I was conceived against my mother's will are some fears that have haunted me since my early years in public school. The students there taunted me with accusations of things like that. They called it, 'having bad blood.' 'Why else would you be adopted?' they taunted. They also taught me the word *illegitimate*. I hated and feared that word. Mom has helped me a lot with these fears, but sometimes, like today, they come back."

Sarah looked at him with understanding in her eyes. "Have you ever thought of searching for your birth parents?" she asked.

"Sometimes, but I'm not ready to do that yet. I guess I'm not ready for what I might find."

As they talked, neither Andy nor Sarah was aware of the cold wind blowing intensely or of the fine snow sifting down outside. But when Andy went to leave, he realized it was unsafe to travel home. "I'll fix a hot breakfast before you leave at daylight," Sarah promised, and when he came downstairs in the morning, Andy was greeted by a warm fire, hot coffee, and a plate of fried potatoes, ham, and eggs.

One lone ribbon of buggy tracks marked the deserted, snow-shrouded road on which Andy's horse and buggy seemed to be the only one brave enough to venture. Several times his horse floundered through a deep drift across the road, but each time the buggy rolled through the snow, and they kept going.

"I should have stayed at the Rabers," Andy said to himself. He peered out into the solid path of whiteness ahead. "I had no idea the roads would be this snow-covered, and I'm not even halfway home!" The road wound through a dense, wooded area where the snowdrifts were deeper, and Andy wondered how much farther he would be able to travel. Coming to a dip in the road, he could see he was in trouble. "Might as well stop at that farmhouse," he decided when a lane to a nearby farm veered off to his right. He recognized it as an Amish farm, but he didn't know the people who lived there.

"Some morning to be out, young man!" The farmer opened the farmhouse door and called to Andy before he had his horse stopped. "Just unhitch your horse, put him in the barn, and come in," he welcomed.

Andy found it hard to be around strangers, but today he had no option. Being tired from the short night and early morning rising, he accepted his host's offer to rest in an upstairs bedroom.

While Andy caught up on sleep in the safe shelter of a

stranger's home, his mother at home was growing increasingly worried. "Keep Andy safe. Lord, keep Andy safe," became her constant prayer as she mechanically did her morning's work.

Two o'clock, where is he? Fanny was alarmed. *I will walk over to cousin Dora's,* she finally decided. Her non-Amish cousin had a car and should be able to help.

"I will be glad to go see where your son is, Fanny," Dora said as she donned a coat and boots. "It's no problem. I need to pick up a few groceries and will just drive out to the Rabers first and see if I can hurry him along home. He is probably warming his feet at their fire and not thinking about his mama at home worrying!"

Dora did not need to drive all the way to the Rabers. Meeting a lone, oncoming buggy, she slowed to a crawl. Recognizing Andy, she rolled down her window and called, "Better get home fast, Andy! Mama's about to have a heart attack; she is that worried!" Dora waved and went on her way to town, glad all was fine.

Well, Fanny, his mother scolded herself when Andy's horse finally trotted up their lane. *Mark tells me not to worry, and I shouldn't, but how do I keep from it?* Her boys were dearer to her heart today than when she had held them in her arms. Soon they would leave home and she would have to give them up, and she didn't know if she was ready.

That summer Andy stood beside the closed casket of his sixteen-year-old cousin who had been killed in a farm accident.

Young Joel King, in the prime of youth, had entered

eternity. His father, Uncle John, owned a little hobby farm to give his boys a taste of farming which they could not acquire from his wood shop business. They had borrowed a neighbor's hay baler because theirs was not working.

"I watched it happen and couldn't do a thing," Uncle John told the circle of relatives. "The horses were hitched to the baler, ready to go, when I needed to help the younger boys put on a bicycle chain. Suddenly, the horses spooked and took off running. Joel shot off after them. I'm sure his first thought was, 'This can't be happening! Not to the neighbor's baler!'

"The horses ran as fast as they could uphill past the barn, but Joel is a fast runner and was gaining on them. I saw him get a burst of speed and get onto the fore cart. I saw him reach for the lines." Then Uncle John bowed his head, and he couldn't go on, as in his mind he saw his son slipping and falling to the left, and then the big baler wheel bumping up over his head. He saw Joel being dragged as he ran to save his son. "He was dragged six feet," he finished, his voice thick with emotion.

Raising his head he continued, and this time his voice held strength and conviction. "But as I saw it happen, it seemed to me God was saying, 'I have a stake planted here for Joel. He can't go past it. His time on earth is over.' It seemed Joel had to make a last effort to meet that place where God was waiting to take him home. That assurance makes Joel's passing easier to bear."

A New Home 14

1986

"Today we will be published to be married! It seems too good to be happening to me!" Andy beamed at his bride-to-be. They were making plans for their upcoming wedding, which would be in just ten days.[1]

"We have so much to decide! I've been working on a list of friends to ask to help and choosing what colors I want the girls to wear. It's all written down in my tablet." Sarah smiled as she handed Andy a tablet with bold, fancy lettering across the front:

WEDDING PLANS for
MR. and MRS. ANDY KING-to-be

Andy scanned the neatly-recorded names under titles of duties. He turned the page to find more names. On another page, there was a to-do list complete with day-to-day jobs and the list of food needed to feed the wedding guests.

"Mom thought we should plan on food for three hundred guests. The food I have listed here is enough for both meals the day of the wedding, dinner and supper."

"This is a lot of food!" Andy whistled, reading down the list in Sarah's neat handwriting.

---

[1] Amish couples in this district did not usually attend church the Sunday they were published to be married.

50 pounds ham

65 pounds chicken

30 pounds bologna

30 pounds Swiss cheese

1 crate celery

16 heads lettuce

10 kettles mashed potatoes

15 loaves bread

4 gallons gravy

12 double batches date pudding

16 bowls carrot salad

20 pounds bananas

20 pounds grapes

1 case Rich's topping

2 gallons pineapple (1 crushed, 1 tidbits)

6 two-and-a-half pound bags of mixed vegetables

4 gallons potatoes (for potato salad)

13 angel food cakes

10 loaf cakes

3 quarts French dressing

1 gallon salad dressing

40 pies

300 blocks Goshen Dairy ice cream

"Think we'll have enough?" he teased. "You're very organized, Sarah. Have you been planning since fall?"

She smiled at him. It was fall when Andy had asked her to be his wife. "Probably," she said shyly.

Four days until my wedding! Andy's whistling didn't help his horse slow down, but he didn't care. Let Ginger run! The road was practically deserted this early Saturday morning, and Ginger needed the workout. *I do want her fully broken before the wedding. She is going to be one good horse!*

Andy and Ginger made excellent time in getting to the Rabers. He had wanted to arrive before breakfast so he would be ready to work when the wedding helpers arrived. Sarah had said the day would be a busy one, and he was ready to begin.

"Mom, we forgot to get red food coloring!" Sarah wailed as she gathered the ingredients for making pie filling. "I can't believe I forgot to write it on my list! Naomi will be here in half an hour, and she won't be able to get started!"

"I'll take Ginger and go to town," Andy offered. "She had a good run over here but also a good rest. Breaking a horse calls for a lot of exercise, and it won't hurt her one bit."

Ginger covered the three-mile trip into town in record time. After buying the food coloring, Andy glanced quickly at the saddle. "Looks tight enough to me," he murmured as he rubbed Ginger's sweaty neck. "She's standing quiet and doesn't seem too winded. I think she's ready to make the run back."

Ginger seemed to agree with him, pulling at the bit as Andy mounted the saddle. As soon as they left town, Andy let her go. He loved the smooth rhythm of her flying hoofs clicking on the blacktop and the flow of her mane streaming with the wind. Leaning forward in the saddle, Andy suddenly felt it slip. The slip spooked Ginger, and soon Andy was fighting both a runaway horse and a loose saddle.

Faster and faster Ginger raced. Andy was powerless to control her as he fought to stay on the slipping saddle. A sickening thought flashed through his mind. *A funeral instead of a wedding?* He spotted a bridge ahead and feared the worst. *Look for a grassy spot!* The thought jolted his numb mind. There was a patch of grass just before the bridge, and Andy tumbled into it.

"Are you okay? Should I call the ambulance? Are you all right?" A girl's frantic voice aroused him, and he looked up to see someone standing over him.

Andy tried to answer but had trouble getting his breath, let alone talking.

"You were knocked out. Your horse is standing just down the road," she babbled, relieved to find him awake. "Are you all right?"

Andy didn't look all right with the mud and blood around his mouth, but neither did he seem to be seriously hurt. The girl had come out to the road to mail a letter when the horse and rider went tearing past. She had watched the rider fly off and heard the thud as the runaway horse slowed, wheeled around, and came to a stop not far from their lane.

Andy sat up and shook his head to clear the fog. "Ouch!" he winced.

"I need my glasses," he said thickly when he could talk.

"Here they are." The girl handed him the twisted frames.

"Where's my horse?" he asked with one thought foremost in his mind. *I must get back to Sarah. She needs the food coloring. I must hurry back.*

"Just back of you, standing by that building," she assured him as he stood up. Andy felt woozy, but he tried to act as normal as possible as he walked with her to his horse.

"Are you sure you should be riding?" the girl questioned as

he stuffed his twisted glasses into the saddlebag. Tightening the saddle he grimaced, then stiffly swung his leg up and over until he was safely in the saddle.

"I'm fine," he replied, not looking fine at all. He didn't realize how his pale, banged-up face scared the girl watching him. "Thanks." The word came out slurred.

Andy kept Ginger to a walk on the way back to the Rabers. He felt thickheaded. The longer he was on the saddle, the worse he felt, but Andy had one thought: *Sarah is waiting for the red food coloring. I must get back. I must get back.*

"Andy!" Sarah grabbed the doorframe. Her knees wanted to buckle, and she felt like passing out. The mud, blood, and grass accentuated his colorless face, giving him a haunted, frightening appearance. "What happened?" she gasped. Only when Andy looked into a mirror did he realize why seeing him had been such a shock to her.

"But I can't go to the doctor!" he argued. "I'll be fine. I have to help get ready for our wedding!" But Andy's pounding headache and Sarah's tears finally convinced him to go. When the neighbor came to drive him to the doctor, he insisted that Sarah should stay and help at the house.

"All right," Sarah consented. He did look better now that he was cleaned up. Everyone was worried about the bump on the back of his head, but since he was willing to go to the doctor, she felt better.

"You were fortunate, young man; all I find is a slight concussion along with a few scratches and bruises and a lost tooth. When you get home, go straight to bed and rest."

"I can't, Doc. My wedding is in three days, and I need to

help with the work."

"Young man, you are going home to bed! If you don't, there may not be a wedding. Do you understand? Head trauma is serious. Until you promise to go home and rest in bed, I can't let you leave my office." The doctor's stern talk shook Andy up, and he promised to obey orders.

Coming out into the waiting room, Andy met an acquaintance who was waiting for an appointment. Andy gave him a nod and a crooked smile.

Mr. Burg looked startled. "What have you been doing to yourself? Trying to keep from saying *yes* on your big day? Afraid Sarah might change her mind?" He chuckled but grew sober when Andy told him what had happened.

"Count your blessings and take it easy, young man. Take it really easy these next couple of days."

Andy spent all afternoon in bed. By late afternoon the work list for Saturday was completed without his help, and it did look like a wedding was going to take place. The buggy shed had been turned into a kitchen with three gas cook stoves installed and ready to begin cooking. All the dishes, kettles, roasters, and utensils they would need, from serving ladles to paring knives, had been borrowed and lay in neat rows on tables set up in the temporary kitchen.

The barn where the wedding service would be held sat swept and empty. Benches would be set up Monday morning when the church bench wagons became available.

Furniture had been moved out of the living, dining, and kitchen areas of the house, and tables for the wedding dinner were in place. The corner bridal table was finished. Two eight-foot tables met in the corner with a small square table filling in the corner gap. A dark blue lace fabric covered the snowy white tablecloth beneath, enhancing the dainty, embossed edging of Sarah's chinaware set from Andy. A clear glass footed bowl for fruit, along with one tiered candleholder, decoratively painted with blue flowers, sat in the center of each table.

"I love it!" Sarah whispered to herself before she covered her china settings with another tablecloth. "Our table is beautiful!"

Monday passed in a blur as one job after another was finished. The cooks had kettles of peeled potatoes ready to cook and mash early Tuesday morning. Chicken was thawing in containers where it had been placed several days before after being cleaned and frozen. Sliced meat and cheese, carrot and fruit salad, and other perishables waited in a rented gas refrigerator. Shelves lining one wall in the temporary kitchen were loaded with angel food cakes, loaf cakes, pies hot out of the ovens, and date pudding waiting for its final mix.

Backless church benches spaced in even rows filled the barn where the three-and-a-half hour service would be held. Rows of long narrow tables with more backless church benches were set up in the house in preparation for the next day's guests. By suppertime all was ready for the wedding, the day's helpers had left, and only the bride's family and groom-to-be sat down to a simple supper. Tomorrow's workday would start at 4:30 a.m. when the people who would fry the chicken arrived. By 7:00, the cooks and all the other helpers would come, and though the service would begin at 8:30 a.m., they would only leave the kitchen at 11:00 to witness the ceremony.

Sarah gave a happy sigh as she went upstairs to her bedroom. Everything was ready for tomorrow. Their wedding day! Tomorrow she could wear her new dark blue dress hanging in the closet. She and her two attendants would wear a white cape and apron over their blue dresses. Going to the closet, she took out her wedding dress. Lifting it high above her head, she gave it a twirl, listening to the soft swish as it fell in folds and caught the gleam of lamplight against its soft satiny finish.

"Imagine! Tomorrow I will be a married woman, married to the best, kindest man in our county, or in the whole world, I'm sure!"

Tuesday morning dawned warm and sunny. *Lord, what a beautiful day for us!* Andy's heart sang. Never had his Sarah looked as beautiful as she did that morning with the sunlight dancing through the tree branches above them. Together they sat outside the building, greeting friends and loved ones who had come to the wedding.

Counseling with the ministers before the service heightened the couple's awareness of the sacredness of the vows they would be repeating before the church and God. Andy felt the weight of his responsibility as husband and leader in the home they would be establishing that day. He felt unworthy of Sarah's love, and he determined in his heart to be the best husband possible. While the couple was meeting with the ministers, the guests took their seats. Men's benches faced the women's with a narrow aisle between the two. All the ordained men sat on the first bench of each side. The bishop and the two ministers who were counseling with Andy and Sarah had places reserved for them on the one bench. Next were chairs reserved for the bridal party. Three chairs for the bride and her two attendants were on the women's side, and opposite them were three chairs for the bridegroom and his two friends.

Singing filled the barn as all the guests waited in expectation for the bridal party to enter. To the four non-Amish neighbors invited to the wedding, it seemed strange to begin a wedding service without the bridal party, but they enjoyed the forty-five minutes of slow, harmonious congregational singing in German.

"It sounds so sacred, I wish I knew what they were singing," the one neighbor lady whispered to the other, who nodded in agreement.

"It's my first time at an Amish wedding," she returned. "Very beautiful and solemn."

By 9:30 the bishop and two ministers who had been with Andy and Sarah filed in. Then on the fourth verse of the song that was being sung, the verse that signaled their entrance, the bridal party entered in single file. Through the open barn doors walked one of the groomsmen. Behind him was a bridesmaid followed by the bridegroom, the bride, another groomsman, and another bridesmaid. The girls were dressed in navy blue dresses, white capes, and plain, long, white aprons without strings. They also wore black caps while every other lady in the congregation wore white caps.

"Notice the black caps?" the one neighbor whispered to her friend. "I was told that single girls wear black caps instead of white for every church service while married women wear white all the time. Only at weddings do the girls in the bridal party wear black, and all the other single girls wear white. The bride will change to a white cap before the wedding dinner."

"Thanks," the lady beside her mouthed with a faint smile. She was observing the children. She marveled at how well-behaved they were. *The babies do cry, and I see small children fussing, but they don't throw tantrums,* she thought.

While the three couples took seats on the chairs facing each other on this beautiful morning of May 6, 1986, thirty-four-year-old Jan [O'Connor] Harding had no idea that her firstborn son was very much alive. The girl who had become a mother almost twenty-one years earlier did not know that her son was the groom at a packed Amish wedding, and that she was about to become a mother-in-law.

At 11:00 a long line of ladies, the cooks and the other helpers, filed in quietly and filled almost three of the empty benches on the women's side. Each wore short, white aprons with strings.

Twenty minutes later the bride and groom rose and walked to where the bishop stood. It was time to say the wedding vows.

After the vows had been said, the congregation knelt in prayer. Joy filled Mark King's heart as he prayed. He thought of the blessing that had come from their choice to adopt. Today he was performing his son's wedding ceremony. There was warmth in his voice as he prayed.

". . . These two stand prepared before thee, O God, to begin and establish matrimony. Do thou open the eyes of mercy over them. Glorify and bless them and grant them thy divine grace, so that their hearts and minds will be directed to thee alone in their undertaking to seek thy divine honor. . . . We ask this for them, O God and Father, through thy dearly beloved Son, Jesus Christ our Lord . . ."

After praying, he took the hand of the bride and placed it in the hand of the bridegroom saying, "The God of Abraham, and the God of Isaac, and the God of Jacob be with you and help you and give His blessings richly unto you, and this through Jesus Christ, Amen."[2]

Andy's heart throbbed with love for his father as he listened to the prayer. How thankful he was for the love, training, and godly example he had received from his parents. Because of them, he was given the opportunity to win the love of his dear, sweet bride.

Fanny cried silent tears of both joy and sorrow. Twenty-one years had flown by too quickly. Such a short time with their son, and now he was beginning a home of his own. "Bless our dear children, bless them," she prayed as she wiped her tears. She smiled as the beaming couple returned to their chairs for the final words of admonition.

Quietly the cooks and their helpers filed out, followed by the bride's family. In a half hour the service would conclude, and the guests would be hungry. The cooks and helpers had a wedding meal to complete.

It was after 10:30 that evening when Andy and Sarah opened the last gift. Guests had thinned out, and only youth friends were milling around when suddenly the barn's metal roof was hammered with pelting rain. A blast of wind swept through the open double doors, scattering wrapping paper

---

[2] Prayers taken from *Our Heritage, Hope, and Faith,* pp. 247-248.

and ribbon across the wooden floor. Lightning flashed and thunder cracked above the roar of the downpour.

Several boys struggled to close the doors, but the wind's strength pushed the doors inward and they gave up, moving back from the entrance, out of the blowing rain. The girls scrambled to move the gifts to a side table.

Then, as suddenly as the storm had blown in, it subsided, leaving raindrops pinging on the roof.

"Some squall that was!"

"We certainly didn't expect that today!"

Before midnight all the guests had left except the bridal party. As was customary, the bridal party would remain overnight at the bride's home and help with cleanup the next day. Tomorrow the women would wash stacks of dirty dishes while the men would load chairs and tables onto the church trailer, dismantle the temporary kitchen, and return borrowed things.

Early Married Life 15

1986-1992

A ndy and Sarah moved into a mobile home that Mark had bought and placed on a small piece of land at the end of Mark and Fanny's lane. Though Andy had slowly increased his herd of milk cows, he was thankful to bring in extra income by working part-time making buggy shafts at a nearby buggy shop.

In August of 1987, a delightful, bright-eyed girl named Rachel joined their household. As Sarah held and nursed their newborn child, Andy was overcome with an intense yearning to have experienced the bond he knew was being formed between his wife and their child. Sarah watched the grief sweeping across her husband's face and knew he was thinking of his rejection as a baby.

Sarah did not understand all of Andy's feelings about this even though she tried. To her it was somewhat of a mystery. She had discussed it with Andy's mother, who told her, "Andy still bears the scars of his rejection at birth. He did not receive love as a newborn baby. He grew slowly and nearly died several times, possibly due to the lack of love."

Sarah knew Andy loved his adoptive parents, and they loved him as their own. She loved Andy with her whole heart, and he loved her in the same way. It should have been enough, but somehow, a piece of her husband would always be missing unless . . . Sarah thought it would help him to find out about his roots, yet she wanted him to be the one to decide. All she could do was accept and love him as his mother did. *That is easy*, she thought and smiled at the love she saw in her husband's eyes as he tenderly stroked his daughter's downy head.

Fourteen months later tiny Sara Kate arrived, and the Andy King household numbered four. When their third baby, Esther, joined her sisters just two years later on October 20, 1990, their little house trailer was bursting at the seams, but a home of love can always make room for one more.

One month and a day after Esther's birth, the local newspaper displayed a picture of an accident with the following caption: "One killed, three injured." A news clip beneath gave several brief details.

"Fatal accident scene: A car driven by Gary F. Dahamel was stopped at the stop sign when a truck reportedly failed to stop and struck the car. A passenger, Jan Mack, 38, of Wythbridge, died in the rear seat of Gary Dahamel's car."

Looking at the obituaries, a person would have read this brief entry:

"Jan Harding Mack died Wednesday, November 21, 1990, from injuries sustained in an automobile accident near Cliveton. She was a member of the Church of the Nazarene."

Andy King did not read the newspaper. If he had seen

the picture of the accident and read the obituary, the name Jan Harding Mack would have meant nothing to him. It would be years before Andy learned of the tragic event that unfolded less than an hour from his farm.

"But, Aunt Jo, where are you taking us?" Allison Harding yelled above the roar of the noisy old truck. Aunt Jo had been waiting at the curb when Allison and her older brother Brent had walked out of school. "You kids get in," she had demanded without explanation.

"Grandmother's house," came Aunt Jo's terse answer before she cursed, downshifted, and slammed on the brakes to avoid hitting a car backing out of a driveway in front of them.

Reaching Grandmother's house, she pulled over but kept the truck idling. "Your mom has been in an accident. You will be staying here." Her fingers drummed the steering wheel as she stared out between the cracks in the windshield, waiting for the two motherless children to get out. Roaring the car's engine, she swung back out onto the street without looking back, cursing in grief at the rottenness of life.

Brent and Allison were used to being passed around and spending time at different houses with various adults. The man who was married to their mother now was neither Allison's nor Brent's birth father. It was not unusual for them to stay for a length of time at their grandmother's house, so they asked no questions. Neither of them asked much about the accident. No one told them their mother had died, no one mentioned a funeral, until several weeks later when Allison asked, "Grandmother, how long is Mom going to be gone?"

"Allison, she died in the accident," Grandmother retorted bluntly and bitterly, unmoved by the stunned expression on her granddaughter's face.

"Died?" Allison tried to process the shocking news. "Mom died?" she asked again, hoping she had not heard right.

"You heard me the first time, Allison. She was killed in the car accident. There is nothing you or I can do about it. Don't worry; you will go on living with me."

Grandmother's words did not soften the blow to nine-year-old Allison's heart. Running from the room, she threw herself onto the bed, sobbing wildly at the knowledge that her mom would never come back.

Marsha O'Connor rubbed her temples. She was still tired from working late at the bar, cleaning up shattered glass mugs after a brawl erupted. *What a mess it had been! Good thing they got the two men quieted down before the cops came. It never bodes well for the establishment when a fight breaks out, and the last thing I need is a cut in customers, especially since Jan's kids were dumped in my lap!*

Allison's cries grated on her nerves, but Marsha did pity her and wanted to do her best for her. Rising wearily from her chair, she went to see if she could make Allison stop crying.

"You could visit your mom's grave," she stated as the inspiration hit her.

"Could I, Grams? Really?" Allison's tears dissolved. She

had never visited a grave.

Visiting the grave and seeing the marker helped to soothe Allison's pain at the loss of her mother. Allison loved the walk along the curved walkway in the graveyard. The various styles of headstones and flower arrangements intrigued her. Something about the quiet peace surrounding her mother's resting place soothed her troubled heart.

"Church of the Nazarene," Allison read the words on the sign as they slowed down for the corner.

"Your mom used to attend there," Marsha said as she braked for stopped traffic.

"Really?" Allison asked as she gazed at the corner church.

"Yeah, but I don't think she went there for a long time, so you probably don't remember that," said Marsha.

Allison continued reading the sign: "Sunday school classes: 9:20 a.m. All ages. Everyone welcome."

"Did you see that sign, Grams? Could I go, Grams?"

"Go where, child?" her grandmother asked with unusual tenderness. Visiting her daughter's grave had softened the hard, unemotional shell she had erected for survival in the harsh, cruel world she had known since childhood. Most of the time Marsha knew no other way to live but to hand back to those around her the same toughness she experienced in life.

"The church sign back there says all are welcome. I want to go to the classes. May I, Grams?" Allison's wistful pleading stirred the dormant embers of love in Marsha's heart. A lump formed in her throat, and she could not answer.

"May I?" Allison persisted.

"Yes," came the gruff reply, and Allison's beaming face

caused the glowing embers of love to burst into a tiny flame.

Though Andy and Sarah King were completely unaware of what had just happened in the lives of Andy's family members, they, too, were experiencing the sorrow of parting. Dear Grandma Yoder died unexpectedly during her sleep and was laid to rest beside her husband.

That summer Andy and Sarah moved into the big farmhouse. With both Grandpa and Grandma Yoder gone, Andy's parents were free to move into the vacant Dawdy house.

Allison Harding 16

1993

Twelve-year-old Allison Harding's delight knew no bounds as she sailed back and forth on the rope swing. Giving a hard pump, she tilted her head back and stretched out her toes as far as possible, just missing the leaves hanging from the branch above. Again and again she tried to reach them, but each time her toes came within a hair's breadth of the leaves.

"I could live here always, Aunt Nora!" she called out in a singsong voice as her great-aunt walked over to her. "It's like living in a park, only better!"

This day was a rare treat. Allison was not used to living in the country with a big yard to play in. The smell of leftover charcoal and grilled hamburgers from the noon cookout mingled with the heady scent of the nearby clover field.

As Nora watched her sister's granddaughter swinging, she reflected on the differences between her life and Marsha's. Though they were sisters with the same tumultuous upbringing, their marriages had placed them in opposite circumstances. Nora had never needed to work away from home to support the family, while Marsha always had. Church was very important to Nora and her husband, while Marsha had never had time for church.

Marsha's life followed closely in the footprints of their childhood. They had grown up with an abusive father. Nora shuddered as she remembered one of the worst things that had happened to them as children. One day their father had loaded the whole family into their beat-up station wagon and had hauled everyone out to California. On arriving, he had dumped them off at a cheap motel and disappeared, letting them fend for themselves.

But we survived! Even if we had to work long and hard! Nora's mind lapsed back in time as she recalled her aching back and shoulders as they sweated under the hot sun. They had picked seasonal fruits and vegetables as they followed the local migrant pickers. It took months of scrimping to save the money for return train tickets to Pennsylvania. She shook her head as if to clear away the cobwebs of unpleasant memories she would rather forget.

Today, as she observed her great-niece swinging with carefree abandon, Nora's heart was wrung with pity for the young girl on the verge of becoming a teenager. Both Allison's mother and grandmother had lived troubled lives; what was in store for happy-go-lucky Allison? A great longing to protect Allison in her innocence had made Nora ask Marsha's permission to talk to Allison. "Go ahead. I can't," had been Marsha's blunt retort.

"I love living here," Allison called as her great-aunt approached the swing. Nora waved in answer and leaned against the tree, waiting for her great-niece to slow down so she could talk to her.

"Allison, I'm going to see if the apples are beginning to ripen in the small orchard beside the clover field. Want to come?"

"I've never picked apples from a tree! Do you think I can?" Allison jumped off the swing, ready for another new adventure.

"We'll pick at least one to see how they are ripening, but I doubt if you'll want to eat a green apple. The reason I wanted to check the apple trees was so I could have a chance to talk to you alone." Her great-aunt smiled pleasantly, and she started without preamble. "Are you aware, Allison, that your mom had a baby boy?"

"Of course! She had Brent!" *That's a silly question*, Allison thought. *Everyone knows about Brent!* He had moved out of Grandmother's house as soon as he turned sixteen and was enrolled in an alternative education program.

"No, another baby boy." Aunt Nora's eyes darkened with sadness. "When your mom was about your age, she had a baby boy. Allison, I want to encourage you to study hard at school so you can graduate with good grades. If you do that, there are always scholarships available to help you finance college. Leave boys alone, focus all your energies on school, and you will never be sorry."

Allison didn't even hear her great-aunt's advice. Her mind was too busy absorbing the shocking news. *A baby at my age! Why didn't Mom ever tell me? A baby at my age!*

"Where is he?" she demanded aloud.

"Allison, the baby didn't live." Nora let out a long slow sigh before continuing. "When your grandmother went to bring the baby home, they told her he was born early and had mental disabilities and was blind. They told her he never had a chance. When your mother came home from the hospital, she struggled a lot. She spent some time in a mental hospital.

"I asked your grandmother if I could talk to you, Allison, and she wanted me to tell you this. She has not had an easy life and finds it hard to express her feelings or talk of important things. I know your grandmother grieved for your mother's baby. I know she grieves for your mother, and I know she wants you to have good growing up years instead of the turmoil your mother went through. It takes all your grandmother's energy to work. When she comes home at night, she doesn't have time to mother you, but she is doing her best." Aunt Nora's smile wrapped Allison in warmth she was not used to.

"Your mother loved you, Allison. You were her bubbly sunshine." Aunt Nora said quietly, becoming lost in thought as she gazed across the clover field.

Allison scuffed her sandal back and forth in the grass. She thought of her mom and the things Aunt Nora said. She thought of her mother's grave in the quiet cemetery. She thought of her dead brother and wondered where his grave was. Suddenly she blurted, "Where is the baby's grave?"

Aunt Nora looked down at her great-niece, startled at the unexpected question. *I wonder too; I have always wondered,* she wanted to answer, but instead she said, "No one knows. No one was notified of the baby's death."

A queer feeling settled over Allison. She never forgot the conversation with her great-aunt. Every time she visited her mother's grave, she thought of a brother somewhere without a grave. It bothered her. She wanted to find it. She felt sad knowing she had a brother in a grave that no one had ever visited. *Someday I will find his grave,* she vowed.

God's Protecting Hand

17

1993-1994

"Sarah, something has been weighing on my mind lately." Andy had purposely lingered at the table to talk to his wife. "What do you think about having morning and evening prayers together as a family? Do you think the children are old enough? Rachel does start school this fall."

"It's fine with me." Sarah answered without hesitating. Her father had never had family prayers at their home, but if her husband wanted to, she was willing. "It is a new thought to me, but it is a good one. Our girls sure have a wonderful father!"

"Children, we are going to kneel for morning prayer before we leave the breakfast table," Andy told them the next day. His heart burned with the responsibility of guiding his children in the ways of God. Three little girls with eager, shining eyes slipped off their bench and knelt down beside it with their hands folded reverently under their chins as their father audibly said a morning prayer.

It warmed Andy to have his family accept the change, and he knew God was blessing his decision when the girls begged to carry the Bible to him each evening when they were ready for bed. He tried to explain the short Bible reading in a way that his girls could understand.

The girls loved kneeling down and listening to him pray. They loved listening to Andy's deep voice rising and falling with the words. Though they didn't understand the meaning, they caught the love in their daddy's tone as he recited the evening prayer:

"Be merciful, beloved heavenly Father! Because thou hast allowed us to enjoy the bright light of the sun so that we should honestly walk according to thy divine will, we thank thy holy name and beseech thee that thou wouldest forgive us what we have this day greatly neglected and have dealt against thy will, which sins we willingly confess.

"Do thou in mercy grant that we may lie down to rest under the shadow of the wings of thy divine grace, being shielded and protected from all the wiles of the enemy who goes about us day and night, so that we may gratefully make use of this night's rest, and at all times be mindful of the coming of thy dear Son, through whom we pour out this prayer before thee and pray, 'Our Father which art in heaven, hallowed be thy name. Thy kingdom come. Thy will be done in earth, as it is in heaven. Give us this day our daily bread. And forgive us our debts, as we forgive our debtors. And lead us not into temptation, but deliver us from evil: For thine is the kingdom, and the power, and the glory, forever. Amen.' "[1]

In February, Andy and Sarah welcomed their fourth daughter, Ruth Edna. Their days were full and overflowing. Andy's small dairy herd was doing well, but added income remained a must. When a fulltime job became available at the lumberyard, he quit the job at the buggy shop.

---

[1] Prayer taken from *Our Heritage, Hope, and Faith*, p. 49.

Working five days a week forced him to push most farm work off till evenings and Saturdays.

Spring arrived with its burst of warm, inviting breezes, and new life seemed to awaken overnight, ready to escape winter's binding dormancy. Lacey, the Kings' newly acquired puppy, ran in circles, yapping in delight as she chased anything that moved. Andy reveled in the task of turning over thick slabs of earth with his new two-way sulky plow. Up and down the field the horses and plow worked steadily, paying no attention to the little dog. They were accustomed to her continuous yapping. Life proved to be an endless flow of excitement to the little high-strung dog the King family had rescued as a pitiful, castoff stray.

"For sure, the faithful eagles are still around!" Andy tipped his head back to watch the mighty pair enjoying the spring day as they floated above, catching the wind currents in an effortless, majestic show.

"Yap, yap, yap!" Lacey's constant barking finally caught Andy's attention. He couldn't see her anywhere, but he could hear her cries coming from over the rise. "Yap, yap, yap!" Her cries increased, taking on urgency. *I should check on her. Maybe she is caught in something,* he thought, and Andy stopped the horses, leaving the plow in the ground. Climbing off the plow seat, he jogged up the rise to see what trouble she had gotten herself into this time. Anything spelling trouble drew Lacey like a magnet.

"Lacey!" Andy scolded when he found the dog frantically barking at nothing but a groundhog hole. "I haven't time to stop and see every new bit of spring!"

Suddenly he heard the horses pop up over the rise behind

him. "Whoa!" he yelled, but the horses did not stop.

Andy broke into a run. The plow started "galloping" behind the horses. Its sharp steel shares hit the ground, and spat out a bite of dirt as the plow catapulted into the air. Then it hit the ground again and started all over with galloping momentum.

"Whoa! Whoa!" Andy yelled, but the horses kept going. Coming out of the field ravine, the horses hit the lane going full tilt, trying to rid themselves of the frightening, bouncing, clanging plow on their heels.

Andy was winded, but he raced on, desperate to stop the runaway horses before they did serious damage to the plow, themselves, or something else. Then the horses and flying plow disappeared.

Mark heard the horses thundering down the field lane toward the barn. He watched helplessly as the plow struck a barn post under the overhanging roof. Breaking off the post made the plow career just enough to let it pass between the barn and another post as the horses slowed a little but kept going. Down the lane to meet the road they flew, but when the two unshod horses hit the pavement, they lost their footing. Skidding across the road, the harnessed horses and plow landed in a tangled heap against the embankment.

Andy! Where is Andy? Mark started running toward the field as memories of nephew Joel's death flashed through his mind. He wasn't worried about the horses; his concern was for his son. Then he saw Andy. *My son! He's running! He's not hurt! Sarah still has her husband!* Thankfulness welled up in his grateful heart, and he slowed to meet his son.

"Dad, where are the horses?"

"Son, are you all right?" Their questions became tangled up in each other as Andy worried about the horses, and his father worried about his son.

It took a bit of talking to quiet the horses and a great deal more time to untangle them. The harness was torn and damaged, but that was a trivial loss. The men breathed a prayer of thankfulness when the horses stood quietly again, not visibly harmed. Even the colt Andy was breaking for someone else and had put between his two workhorses was unhurt.

Later that day Andy did find a twist in the plow. Even though it left a crooked furrow, he continued to use it, a reminder to him of God's protecting hand.

More Protection

18

1995-2000

Eight months after Ruth Edna celebrated her first birthday, baby Mary joined the family. Then after three more years went by, five excited girls were awed by the arrival of Johnny. Finally they had a little brother of their very own!

While the King household of girls thrilled over each of Johnny's new developments, Allison Harding, now a student in high school, was excited to discover she had free access to the library computers. She loved having information at the tip of her fingers. She loved being able to search and receive answers. One day after she was finished with her work, Allison went online to see what she could discover when she typed: "How do you find where a gravesite is located?" She had never forgotten the long ago talk with Aunt Nora about her other brother.

In seconds the information popped up. Allison scanned the websites eagerly. Logging off the computer, she felt optimistic. "I've got to talk to Grams tonight! This might actually be easy!"

Armed with the name of the hospital and date of birth from her grandmother, Allison returned early the next morning to complete her search. "No death recorded."

"Not available." "Unable to find." She chewed on her bottom lip as every route she pursued came up blank.

"This doesn't make sense!" she fumed as she exited the library. "If there was a death, the hospital would have the record. We don't live in the dark ages. Babies don't just evaporate into thin air!" But it did seem like that had happened to Baby Boy O'Connor.

Allison's failure to find information drove her to dig deeper into the mystery surrounding the death of her unknown brother. Somewhere, a little untended grave needed to know it was not forgotten.

One day she called her great-aunt. "Aunt Nora, I need to talk to you!" Allison said. "Several weeks ago I went online to try to find the gravesite for Mom's baby, and when I typed in the name of the hospital and birthdate of Mom's baby, there was nothing! It's weird! It's like he never existed!"

Nora shivered. Goosebumps peppered her arms and she took a deep breath. Maybe it was time to tell Allison the doubts she and some of her sisters had always had about the baby's death. "Allison, you aren't the first person to suspect something is not right. We have always wondered what actually happened because your grandmother never received a death certificate. Did the baby die, or was it just the state's way of protecting a handicapped baby born of a minor? Your mother was a ward of the state at that time. That gave the state the liberty to do what it thought was best." Nora hated to upset her great-niece, but if she had questions, now was the right time to talk about the incident.

"Why didn't you try to find out if you suspected something?" Allison asked.

"Your grandmother refused to talk about Jan's baby. Allison, you can't barge into people's lives and do things they aren't ready to do. When this happened, your grandmother was hurting a lot. Try to understand all she had to deal with. She did not need us sisters stirring up further hurt. Though we have thought about it over the years and talked about it among ourselves, I am consoled with the thought that God knew what was best for the baby."

Nora's gentle words only increased Allison's determination to find out the facts. But, before Allison found any further information, and before she had finished high school, she met Rod Bentley. Thinking she was the luckiest girl in town, she dropped out of school to get married. Before the young couple celebrated their first wedding anniversary, they became the parents of a beautiful baby girl.

Allison loved little Robin with a fierce, protective love. She embraced motherhood and, thrilled by her happy life as Rod's wife, she started attending a nearby church. Taking care of her own baby made her think of her mom, and she remembered how her mom had gone to church at some point in her life. Allison wanted Robin to have the best, and to Allison, the best included going to church. Allison enjoyed the emotional worship services she attended. She felt inspired, and her spirit was uplifted as she left the church building with hallelujahs ringing in her ears.

Being a mother made Allison feel close to her own mother, and she loved the feeling. It also wakened the desire to find closure about her other brother's infant death.

Andy and Sarah's family increased to seven children

when baby Jacob was born. One warm fall Saturday afternoon, eight-month-old Jacob would not stop fussing. "Poor baby," Sarah murmured. She kissed his flushed cheek and rubbed his swollen gums with teething gel, hoping it would help him take a longer nap.

"Do you girls have the upstairs bedrooms swept?" she asked.

"Yes, Mom, they are all cleaned," Rachel answered. "And cleaned well!" she added with a grin.

"Please take Jacob upstairs and put him to sleep," Mom instructed. "He certainly is a fussy youngster today!"

That morning Esther had lit a long taper candle and had set it on the bookcase to brighten their clean bedroom. She had put a tissue under the candle holder to catch any drips. "We don't want to mark up our beautiful bookcase," she had informed her sister, Rachel. Esther's eyes had swept lovingly over the prized bookcase holding a cherished collection of storybooks.

"The burning candle makes our bookcase even prettier," Rachel had said with a sigh as she took a longing glance at the straightened books, beckoning to be read.

By now the wick was getting close to the end of the candle. Rachel had forgotten all about it. Holding baby Jacob, she bypassed their room and went to the younger girls' room where there was an extra crib. Singing softly, she rocked sweet, chubby Jacob.

As Rachel sang and rocked, the burning candle in the next room almost burnt itself out, but just before it did, it toppled over. The flame ignited the tissue Esther had placed beneath the holder to catch any drips.

While Rachel rocked and sang, a piece of burning tissue fell behind the polished bookcase. Tiny smoldering flames licked at the bottom edge of the dry, unfinished wood, catching hold of minute, splintery slivers as Rachel lowered sleeping Jacob gently into the crib.

Rachel closed the door and tiptoed out of the room and down the stair steps. "Mom, Jacob's finally sleeping!" she called. "What do you want me to do now?"

"Get the laundry off the line, please. It should be dry," Mom instructed.

Minutes later the quiet afternoon was shattered by a piercing wail coming from the newly-installed smoke detector upstairs. The next moment the downstairs detector emitted its ear-splitting siren, and Sarah King flew upstairs into a cloud of smoke. Snatching crying Jacob out of his bed, she almost fell down the stair steps in her haste. "Take him! All of you go to our spot," she said as she shoved the baby into Rachel's arms. Grabbing both of the fire extinguishers they kept in the kitchen, she flew back upstairs and started blasting the wall behind the bookcase where flames leaped toward the ceiling.

When the smoke alarms went off in the house, Andy was out in the buggy shop hobbling around gingerly. Every step brought a knife-like stabbing pain to his lower back. *Moving those two-by-fours yesterday was a big mistake. How am I to get my work done?* he groused. Then he heard the shrill scream of the newly-installed smoke detector. Seconds later he heard the downstairs alarm. *Why would they both be going off? Are they not set right?* He hobbled over to the shop doorway to see black smoke billowing out of the older girls' open bedroom window. His heart beat violently. He fought down the feeling of helplessness as another shot of intense back pain hit him, taking his breath away. At that instant he saw Rachel running across the yard with the baby while Sara Kate herded the rest of the children to the far garden spot along his parents' fence. That was the safety spot they had drilled into the children as a place to go to in case of a fire. His breath gave way as he struggled toward the house.

Sarah? Where are you? Sarah! Panic pushed his physical pain away until all he felt was each anguished heartbeat pleading, *Sarah, Sarah, Sarah* . . . He didn't remember getting to the house or climbing the stairs. He knew nothing until he saw his dear, soot-covered wife emptying the last extinguisher onto a blackened bedroom wall and ceiling. "Thank you! Thank you, God," his heart cried over and over again.

"I . . . think . . . it's . . . out . . ." she coughed violently between words when she realized her husband was with her. Thick smoke choked her, making it hard to breathe, and she gladly let her husband lead her downstairs and outside. By the time they made it to the children, Grandmother King had awakened from her afternoon nap and joined the anxious children waiting for their parents.

A sober family reentered their home and trooped upstairs to inspect the damage.

"It's my fault, Daddy!" Esther sobbed. "I left the candle burning! The fire started right here where I put the candle. It's my fault! I know it is." She hugged her father in misery as he spoke to her reassuringly.

"Mom!" Rachel's mouth flew open as she pointed to the

once-beautiful bookcase. "The back is all burned! And look at our books! Some of them are burned!"

"This was a close call, a very close call." Andy touched a book still warm from the fire, its edges scorched and crumbly. "Children, God surely protected us this afternoon. To think I complained about spending the money to put these alarms in! God used them to alert Mom to the fire. We still have our house, and none of you children were harmed."

What a mess the small fire made with its smoke damage! The rest of the day was spent in cleaning up and throwing things out. When Andy's father pulled off the charred particleboard behind the bookcase, the adults realized that the house was a standing tinderbox with its old, flaky particleboard walls. This had been very close to developing into an uncontrollable fire.

Later, when Andy lit the pile of particleboard, it ignited with a roar, and he realized again how God had spared their family. It would have been only a matter of minutes until the whole upstairs would have been engulfed in flames. It was too hard to think of what could have happened.

That night before evening prayers, Andy's eyes glistened as he took in the complete family circle. All were safe. "Children, God had His hand of safety over our home today. Let us never forget His mercy as we thank Him."

"Do we have to sleep upstairs, Daddy?" Ruth Edna's chin quivered. Big tears hung on her eyelashes and splashed down before she buried her head in his lap and sobbed, "I'm scared."

Andy hadn't anticipated his children's fear of sleeping upstairs, but seeing his two oldest daughters nod in agreement, he came to a quick decision. "Everyone may sleep down-stairs tonight. How about that?" He stroked his daughter's curly red-brown hair and was rewarded when a small smile appeared on her tearstained face.

Night after night the younger children feared going up-stairs. Making beds on the living room floor became a nightly ritual and continued until Sarah's sister came to help them with fall cleaning.

"I think this is the time for you to consider building an-other house." Andy's dad suggested as the two men tore out more blackened wallboard from the upstairs bedroom. "We are working with an old house that is both too little for your growing family and not structurally worth the money to add onto," he continued.

"When?" Andy asked. "In the spring?"

"Yes, that would give us the whole summer and into fall to finish it. I've been thinking about it. I figure we could have the basement done by early summer and have a work bee for the framing, roofing, and outside walls. Building a house is a lot of work, but I will be able to help, and it will cut down expense if we do most of the finishing work ourselves." Dad's advice and encouragement gave Andy the nudge he needed to start planning.

Temporary patching was done to the upstairs bedroom. The burnt wall was given a coat of white paint to block any lingering smoke smell, and the children moved back into their bedrooms, too excited about building a new house to dwell on their fear of the past fire.

Searching

19

2002-2009

On the last Friday in July, Andy and Sarah King and their eight children boarded the chartered bus enroute to a neighboring state for the annual adoption reunion. Only baby Rose Anna was too little to share the excitement of her siblings.

The yearly reunion was attended by Amish families who had become connected over the years through the common experience of adoption. Some came because they had adopted children, others because they were adopted. Some of those who had been adopted were now married and brought their own families to the reunion. Friends and strangers mingled, renewing old acquaintances or making new ones.

"Hello! My name is Daniel Miller," a stranger introduced himself to Andy. "Do you know Aaron Schwartz?"

"No," Andy answered.

"You look just like him," the new acquaintance said, "and you even talk like him! He's adopted, too."

"Oh, that is interesting!" Andy replied, not thinking much of the incident. But later that same evening another person he had never met came and said to him, "Are you Aaron Schwartz's brother? You certainly look and talk like him!" Andy was startled to be asked the same question twice in one evening. He shook his head. "Well," said the man, "I thought for sure you were!"

Do I have siblings somewhere, waiting to connect with me? Did God send these two strangers to tell me it is time to look into my past? How would I start? Unsettling questions rose to torment Andy, questions he had kept buried and refused to address. *Who would I go to for answers? Or is it best I leave things as they are? Lord, are you telling me it is time to search? In two years Rachel will be sixteen. Will finding my roots make it easier or harder for her?* He couldn't forget Jeremiah Miller. Suddenly, Andy had an overpowering desire to settle the questions that had plagued him all through life instead of pretending they did not exist.

Andy waited until they were at home to share with Sarah the questions he'd been asked at the reunion and the feelings they had stirred up. "How do you feel about me searching for my biological roots?" he asked his wife.

"I have no problem with you searching. I will support you," Sarah encouraged without hesitating.

"We need to pray, Sarah. I need to know if this is what God wants me to do."

"Thy will be done, Lord," he prayed. As he prayed, he also tried to prepare himself to accept no as God's answer, or to accept that he might not have any living blood relatives. He struggled with the thought of accepting no for an answer. The desire to find out about himself was a small flame that grew stronger the longer he prayed and waited.

Several weeks after the reunion, Andy made an appointment with their family doctor. "He's the only person I know who would be able to help me," he confided to Sarah. "If he can't help, I will take that as God's will to let this drop."

"Have you ever helped with a biological search?" he asked his doctor.

"No," came the disappointing answer. Andy felt his heart plummeting, but in the next instant it soared as the doctor added, "But let me give you some phone numbers I have that may help you."

Thank you, Lord, thank you! Suddenly Andy realized how badly he wanted to know about his past. He had always wanted answers, but he had feared what those answers might be. Now there was no turning back. Whatever God allowed him to find out, he would accept.

"I hope these will help you." The doctor handed him a paper with two phone numbers written on it. Andy couldn't wait. The numbers seemed to burn in his pocket. His horse seemed to dawdle the whole way home from town. He tried to relax, but his hands gripped the reins, refusing to cooperate. As soon as the horses turned into their lane, he stopped at their phone hut by the road. Suddenly, his feet felt like bricks and the buggy seat a vise grip. *Was he ready?* Knowing his wife was supporting him and praying for him gave him courage to enter the phone hut and dial the first number.

"I'm sorry, we do only biological searches with a doctor's request for medical reasons," the distant voice spilled out the words into his ear, "but I will give you the number of the Adoption Network. They do searches."

Andy dialed the new number and was immediately connected with a secretary who gave her name as Linda Bellini.

"Do you do biological searches?" he asked her.

"Yes, sir, I would be happy to assist you!" Her positive, enthusiastic response was exciting. *Someone who could help! Someone who could give him answers to his questions!* Andy's mind flashed ahead at the thought.

"Sir, I will be happy to send you the information you will need to begin your search," she explained as she took his address.

Thank you, Lord! Andy felt as light as a soaring eagle when he climbed into the buggy and drove up the lane. That evening he and Sarah went over to talk to his parents. He wanted to know how they felt him about him searching for his biological family.

"I don't have a problem with it," his dad promptly replied. "You know, Andy, though your mother rejected you at birth, God never rejected you. It was His plan for another family, for us, to get the chance to love you."

"I know, Dad. I have never felt rejection from you. I have thanked God over and over for giving me a godly home and parents like you. But I have always wondered, what if I have blood siblings who know about me but don't know how to find me? What if someone does know but doesn't want to find me? I've gone over and over these questions, and only since the reunion have I felt God wanting me to search.

"Mom?" Andy asked when she stayed silent.

"Son, I want to say no, but I can't. I guess I'm afraid you will either find information you may wish you never knew, or not find out anything at all and have your hopes dashed. But I will pray for you, and God bless you, son," she answered with tears in her eyes.

Andy soon found out that a biological search was not finished overnight, nor in a week, a month, or even a year. For him, it would take seven long years. Many times he became discouraged as he waited to receive the information the Adoption Network requested. Months would pass without any tangible progress.

To begin his search, Andy needed to have his case number released. To accomplish this, he had to write a letter of petition to the county judge, asking to have this information released.

When he received a signed letter from the county judge granting permission, Andy was told the next step would be drafting a letter of request to the County Probate Court for release of non-identifying information pertaining to his birth and adoption.

"What does all this mean?" he asked in confusion as he read the letter from the judge. "What do I do when I have no idea what they want?" Sarah hated the disappointment spilling from his questions and the way he sat hunched over the letter spread out before him on the table. Then she thought of the lady who seemed ready to help him when he first contacted Adoption Network.

"What about calling Linda, the lady who seemed willing to help at the beginning?" she asked.

"I'll call her. Exactly. I never even thought of asking her!" Andy rose from the table.

"Let's set up an appointment for next week, and I will help you draft a letter of request to the County Probate Court." Linda's offer was reassuring, giving him something to hold on to in this quest into the unknown.

"Begin your letter by writing, 'Dear Judge Brown:' " Linda dictated at the appointment. She continued to help him with the wording until the finished letter read:

Dear Judge Brown:

My name is Andy King, and I was born on December 23, 1965, in Wilton County and adopted through the Wilton County Children Services Agency, then known as the Child Welfare Board. I was referred to you by the agency for the purpose of requesting that your permission be granted to them to release to me any non-identifying information in my file that is available to me. Below are the questions I would like to have answered if possible:

Linda helped Andy draft thirty-four questions—questions about siblings, his mother's age at his birth, her occupation, nationality, her parents' ages and occupations, his father's age at Andy's birth, occupation, nationality, etc. They finished the letter with:

My hope is that many, if not all, of these questions can be answered by the Children Services Agency with your permission based on the social background and medical history they were given at that time. My adoptive parents are wonderful and totally supportive of my search for information.

Thank you in advance, Judge Brown, for intervening on my behalf in an effort to secure my non-identifying information. I look forward to getting your response.

Sincerely,
Andy King
Adult Adoptee

Month after month passed as Andy waited for a reply. "This feels like an up-and-down journey," he shared with Sarah one evening. "I had no idea it would be this complicated! Should we continue or not?" he added as he rubbed his shoulder. It had been a busy day at work, and the lack of progress in this search added to his weariness.

"We prayed," Sarah reminded him. "Should we just trust God's timing?" Andy smiled. His wife's words encouraged him.

While Andy waited to hear from the Children Services Agency, Linda Bellini was busy searching for him herself. One day he came home to find a phone message from her. Andy immediately dialed the number she had left, wondering if things had come to a dead end.

"Hello, Andy," Linda answered. "I'm glad you called as I have been doing research on your behalf and found some information for you. Are you ready to hear what I have found?"

"Yes, I think I am ready," he replied slowly. As he held the phone receiver he wondered, *Am I really ready?*

"The information I am giving you concerns your mother. Her maiden name was Jan O'Connor. Then her first married name was Jan Harding, and her last married name was Jan Mack. I'm sorry, Andy, to have to relay this news, but in 1990, at the age of thirty-eight, she was killed in an automobile accident." Linda's quiet tone softened the blow as Andy absorbed the blast of information.

"I wish I had something different to tell you, but it is still good to know about your past, right?"

"Yes, Linda," he answered, "that is why we are doing this. Though I wish the news were different, I've had this feeling for a while that maybe she isn't living." *1990,* he thought, *my mother died the year Esther was born.*

"I also found out your mother was a young girl of thirteen," Linda's voice faded into the background as the shocking news registered. *No! It couldn't be! No wonder I was abandoned!* A host of unwanted thoughts flooded his mind as to why a young girl of thirteen had had a baby. Then compassion took over. *Thirteen? Far too young to begin thinking of such a responsibility! Thirteen? His poor mother, what had she gone through?*

"Andy, are you all right?" Linda asked in concern when a lengthy silence followed.

"Just processing the information," he said quietly.

"We will keep searching," she encouraged. "As of yet, I have found no contact number or name of a sibling searching, but if someone is, we will find him."

Andy took a deep breath after they finished conversing. *I will tell Sarah what I have learned, but no one else needs to know for now. Right now it is too painful to share with others,* he decided.

Several more years passed before a big brown envelope

arrived in the King mailbox. All afternoon the family eyed the envelope stamped with the name, Adoption Network, on the return address. Would Dad ever get home from work? The spoken and unspoken question burned and smoldered, growing in intensity, as the clock hands ticked slowly on, refusing to hurry the time they longed to rush.

"Dad's home! Dad's home!" The cry rang through the house as the younger children ran out to meet the van that brought their father home from work. "It came! A huge envelope came for you! It's on the table! Will you show us, too? Can we open it now?" The news and questions tumbled over each other as Andy's children excitedly vied for his attention.

Andy found his own excitement matching his children's when he, too, spied the unopened mail. *At least it is not flat!* Pulling out a chair, he sat down and reached for the mysterious sealed envelope. Suddenly the kitchen became quiet, and looking up into the faces of his dear family, he felt protective. He didn't know what information the papers inside would reveal, but he felt the time had come to tell his children what he already knew about his background.

"Before I open this envelope, I want to tell you something I learned several years ago," he began. "Not everything we will learn about my past will be good. Maybe there won't be anything good at all. Maybe you will be ashamed and wish you didn't know, but remember, God cared about me before I was born, just as God cared about each of you before you were born.

"Whatever we find out in this envelope will make no difference in God's love for you. Think of it this way. Because of God's love and care, He placed me in a loving home with godly parents. Because of that, I can now raise you in the same kind of environment. Children, we are richly blessed!

"Now, I want to tell you what I have already found out about my birth mother.

"She is no longer living. She was thirty-eight years old the year you were born, Esther, and that year she was killed in an automobile accident. She also gave birth to me when she was very young. Too young to be a mother."

Surprise, disbelief, and questions flooded the faces of Andy's girls. "I see your questions, girls. As I told you earlier, not all the things we learn will be good things. Mom and I don't want you to talk to others about the things we are learning about my past. We want to keep the information within our own family. Okay?"

Heads nodded as Andy slit the envelope. He breathed a silent prayer, "Your will be done, Lord." What would he find?

Andy pulled out sheaves of papers, some loose and others with several pages stapled together. He picked up the top sheet. "Physician's Record of Newborn Infant," he read. The next one bore the title, "Hospital Record on Mother and Baby." He sifted through several written pages of his medical records from birth until adoption, his various stays at several hospitals, his eating habits, his foster mother's name, and copies of the letters he had drafted to request information release.

He picked up four sheets of paper containing the non-identifying questions he had asked and the answers to them. Scanning the answer sheet, he was disappointed to see many of them marked unknown or not available. As his girls discussed and giggled over his baby medical records and eating habits, he removed three papers dated 1966 with the headline at the top, "Custody of Child Welfare Board." A blacked-out sentence on the top sheet caught his attention. Flipping it over, he saw another page with more blackened sentences. Curious, he got the flashlight and retreated to the living room to read in privacy.

Wording before the first blackened space read: "The father of this child has not been determined, but it is of more than academic interest that"—and the rest was blacked out. Turning to the other marked page he read: "Parents: Father not determined"—and again it was blacked out. *This doesn't look good.* Andy turned on the flashlight, holding it under the blackened spaces to see if he could read the print behind the black cover-up. A tremor passed through him as he deciphered the hidden wording. His arms sagged, and he wasn't sure if he had the strength to rise from the chair he was sitting in. His spirit groaned, he shut his eyes, but he couldn't shut out the words he had just read. "Help me, Lord God," he pleaded and rose heavily from the chair. Snapping off the flashlight, he took the papers and went into their bedroom where he put them on top of the tall chest. Silently he left the house and headed to the woods, his heart and mind in turmoil.

"Lord," Andy whispered as he wrestled with the devastating information he had uncovered. "Lord," he groaned again under the weight that threatened to destroy his peace. "Help me accept this. I can't do this on my own. I know I prayed thy will be done, but this is a hard thing."

Nature's gentle voices reached out to him, calling to his troubled spirit as they had when he used to come to the woods for solace as a young boy. Taking a deep breath, he inhaled the clean, fresh air. With it came a measure of calmness. Andy looked heavenward, praying for victory, and as he communed with God, God reminded him of the Scriptures that had helped him accept adoption and its stigma.

As he stared at the sky, Andy noticed an eagle circling overhead. Leaning against a tree, he drank in the sight of its magnificent wings dipping, gliding effortlessly. Suddenly the eagle dropped to the earth. Just before meeting the ground, it spread its wings. A terrified squeal echoed across the field as the eagle swooped upward with a rabbit firmly in its talons. A Scripture flashed into Andy's mind. God had asked Job, "Doth the eagle mount up at thy command, and make her nest on high?"[1]

"By God's command, not by anything man does." Andy said aloud. He marveled at the privilege of watching the eagle make a kill. He was humbled that God had allowed him to see this rare spectacle. It seemed that God was reminding him, "Andy, I am in control of what happens in your life. If I care for the eagle, how much more do I care for you?"

Andy returned to the house with a new sense of God's mercy to him. That evening after the children had gone to their bedrooms, he took the papers from the top of the chest. Turning to his wife he said, "Sarah, I think I know who my father may be. Listen to this. 'It is reported that

---

[1] Job 39:27

the mother, after the birth of Baby Boy O'Connor, again became involved with several males and is at present a patient in the state hospital. The father of this child has not been determined, but it is of more than academic interest that . . ." Andy's hand shook as he pointed to the blacked-out ending. "With a light I could make out the words 'he is one of her older siblings.' "

Gathering his wife close, he whispered against her hair, "According to my medical reports I should have cerebral palsy, be practically blind, and have other abnormalities, but I'm normal in every way, am I not?" Sarah could feel the wild beating of her husband's heart and knew what a blow it had been to decipher these words spelling out what he had always feared to be true.

"Dear Sarah, I went back to the woods, and God met my need." Sarah gave silent thanks as she listened to his voice change and vibrate with the message God had revealed to him. He finished by saying, "God knew where I was going, and He knew a couple struggling with infertility. He knew the love I would need throughout childhood. And yes, Sarah, God also knew I needed a tender but strong, supportive wife.

"I thank God for giving me a sound mind and healthy body. I want to live a life of appreciation that shows others that being adopted is truly a blessing. I want to demonstrate that whether a person is adopted or raised by biological parents, a bond with Christ is the most important factor in life."

By the spring of 2009, Andy believed he had received all the information available about his background. Two more sons had been welcomed into the King family. Levi had been born in August 2004, and baby Elijah had just celebrated his second birthday.

Seven years had expired since the 2002 reunion when Andy had been asked twice if he was related to Aaron Schwartz. Not once in the seven-year search had he received any information about a sibling looking for him. "I believe I am an only child," he told his wife, resigned that the brown envelope held all the information he would ever know about his background.

While Andy accepted the end of his search for his biological roots, Allison Bentley had resumed her search for a brother she was sure hadn't died at birth. One Sunday she came home from church and said to her husband excitedly, "Rod, the pastor said something to me when he shook my hand after the service today that I can't stop thinking about. Listen to this!"

"That must have been some service you attended," her husband drawled as he turned down the volume of the baseball game he was watching to hear what she was saying. He and Allison had an agreement. She could attend church all she wanted to if he could stay at home and watch ballgames. But when church was over, he had to turn off the TV, and they would do something fun together with their two girls.

"Rod, it wasn't about the service! If you would only listen," she pouted. "When I shook hands with Pastor Chapland he said, 'Allison, is something going to happen to you?' "

"I was so astonished I couldn't say anything. It was like he knew about this search for my brother that I've been praying about for so long.

"Rod, I think something big is going to happen. The last time I talked to my friend Karen McKay who works at the Children Services Agency, she told me she thought she was onto a breakthrough. Remember, she said there are 'ways of finding out' but she couldn't give me any information? Well, after today I am just waiting for a phone call!"

Several weeks after Allison's experience at church, Andy received an unexpected phone call at work from Linda Bellini.

"Andy," she began without preamble, "sorry to interrupt you at work, but I have a phone number you need to call as soon as you can." Linda tried to talk normally, but she couldn't keep the excitement from creeping into her voice, and Andy caught it.

"What's going on?" he asked.

"Andy, are you sitting down? I have made connection with a biological sister! And that is not all! You also have a grandmother!" Linda couldn't keep the good news any longer but spilled it all out. "And—they both live only forty-five miles from your farm!"

"For sure?" The words escaped Andy's mouth before he realized he'd said anything. It was almost more than he could comprehend. *A sister! A grandmother!* He had to sit down a little to process the information before going back to work.

The time passed slowly until Andy was finally able to go home and talk to Sarah. When he told her the news, she did not hesitate, but said, "You do whatever you think is best. I will support you all the way." Sarah's calm, encouraging words gave Andy the courage to press ahead.

He didn't call the first evening. He felt he needed time to pray and prepare for the call. *How will I approach my sister? Does she know she has a brother? Will she want to talk to me? How will my grandmother feel to hear I want to intrude in her life? No grandmother was mentioned in my reports from the state. But she had to have known her thirteen-year-old daughter had a baby!* There were so many unknowns, but he had gone too far to turn back.

He waited a day before going to their phone hut to call. Dialing the number, he took a deep breath as the phone started ringing. His hand felt weak, and then a female voice answered, "Hello?" The time had arrived.

"Hello. I am Andy King. I am wondering if anyone at this household knows about an adopted sibling."

A wild shriek sounded in his ear before a breathless, "Yes! Yes! I'm Allison Bentley, and I have been looking for a brother born on December 23, 1965. Is that you?"

"That's my birthday," Andy assured her as summer's sunbeams streaming in the window of the phone hut took on a golden hue.

Talking to his sister was easy. Her conversation bubbled from one topic to the next, and when they finally hung up almost forty-five minutes later, Andy felt as though he simply could not digest all the information he had just received.

"My sister's name is Allison." Andy began when he gathered his family together to share the news. "Allison has been searching for a brother off and on since she was seventeen.

When she was twelve, she heard about an older brother who had died at birth, so her first searches were for a grave," he continued.

"I also have a living grandmother, but she, too, thought that I had not lived. Right now my mind is spinning from all that my sister told me. She seemed overjoyed to talk. We did make plans for her to come out to our farm on Labor Day. Oh, I forgot to say that she is married and has two girls."

"What are their ages, Daddy?" Rose Anna asked.

"I think she said ten and five."

"Oh, good! They are close to my age!" she sang out happily at the thought of having new friends.

"Allison said she would call again once she talks to her husband, to let us know if it will suit him to come that weekend."

"Did you tell her you were Amish?" Sarah asked her husband.

"No. I never had the right chance to bring it up," Andy replied.

"I think you should," Sarah persisted. "Just so she knows."

"We'll see," Andy said. But inside, his thoughts ran on. *How can I tell Sarah I'm afraid my sister might back out of meeting me if she knows I'm Amish? I don't think Sarah understands how important it is for me to see someone just once who had the same blood mother I did.*

While Andy waited for Labor Day and the meeting with his sister, Allison found it hard to understand her grandmother. "Grandmother, I'm going to meet my brother whether you like it or not! My brother isn't dead! He is very much alive! He is married, and he and his wife have ten children!"

Allison didn't understand the emotions warring within her elderly grandmother. *Forty-three years of thinking your grandson is dead! That is too hard to accept. Having a wife and ten children! That is even harder.*

The Meeting 20

2009

"Rod! Please!" Allison's nervous voice raised several octaves when he started crossing the solid double lines to pass the dawdling horse ahead of them. "You can't see if anything is coming on the curvy road, and we don't want an accident." She took a deep breath, willing herself to relax. "Sorry, hon," she apologized. "I never dreamed I would be this nervous about meeting my brother. He was easy to talk to on the telephone, but this seems different, to actually see him and meet his family!"

"If it makes you so nervous, we can go home and come another time," Rod offered as he thumped the steering wheel, keeping time to the beat of the music that filled their red Oldsmobile Cutlass.

"Oh, no!" Allison exclaimed. "Rod, I . . . I . . . need to do this!" Her words trailed off as she glimpsed another horse trotting along an adjacent side road. "Why are there so many horses and buggies around here? It looks like the whole country is Amish! I had no idea!"

"Mom! That farmhouse has two horses tied up by the barn!" five-year-old Jenny exclaimed. Allison swiveled sideways, taking in the neat farm buildings surrounded by fields of tall yellow-green corn plants, and the clothesline stretching on and on across the yard. Dark pants and solid-colored dresses marched along its entire length. *Wow!* She sucked in her breath then slowly let it out as two young boys tumbled out the front door, raced across the sweeping veranda, and, in several long jumps, descended the wide front steps of the three-story white house. Both wore dark clothes matching those hanging on the clothesline.

Amish! Allison had never been this close to Amish people before. Her home was just forty-five minutes away, but there were no Amish in the city where they lived. Allison glanced back over her right shoulder and laughed aloud to see both her daughters pressed tightly against the car window.

"It's like watching a movie," Robin grinned at her, "but without talking, just action and music. Weird!" She wrinkled her nose as the horse ahead left definite signs of having been there. "Gross! Swerve, Dad, swerve," she sputtered and gagged.

"Stop it! You're ten years old!" Allison scolded, not sure why she was reacting this way when she felt the same way. *Amish!* Allison's dark eyes widened as she tucked her short hair behind her ears. She looked down at her crisp, tan shorts and new matching striped top. *Amish! Could my brother be Amish? Are we headed to an Amish farm?*

As Rod swung out to pass the buggy, Allison blurted, "What if my brother is Amish?"

"What?" Rod frowned. Flooring the gas pedal, he sped on. Braking hard, he cut back into his lane to avoid the oncoming car and the team of horses pulling a loaded wagon just ahead. "What did you say?"

"What if my brother is Amish?" Allison repeated.

"What makes you think that?" he mumbled with a shrug.

"Rod, look out the window! Amish are everywhere! This whole area is saturated with Amish!

"Don't you girls say one word if they are," she warned, suddenly seized with fierce protection for this brother she was about to meet.

The red Oldsmobile rounded the bend in the road at the end of the King lane and stopped. Andy heard the gears shift and saw the car begin to climb their long, sloping driveway.

"Help me, Lord, to accept whatever this day brings." Andy breathed as each step toward the waiting car increased the tightening emotions warring within him. Time seemed to hang in a balance. The sultry Labor Day heat held the usual hilltop breezes at bay. It seemed as if all nature was holding its breath, waiting, waiting for him to meet, to make contact with someone with whom he shared a blood mother.

To Andy it seemed a lifetime of waiting. It was fascinating to see his sister step away from the car. *His sister!* He drank in the sight of her. *Did they bear any resemblance to each other? Did she look like their mother, or did he? Their mother!* The thought filled him with wonder. *They shared the same birth mother! His sister! A sister to call his own!* For as long as he could remember, he had longed for the time when he would know about the mother who gave him birth. He had dreamed of this time, but never had he thought this privilege would actually be his to experience.

As Andy extended his large work-calloused hand to welcome this newly-arrived sister, he did not think of the differences in their upbringing. His thoughts and eyes were focused solely on his sister's face. Gladness welled up from the depths of his heart when she, too, offered her hand of friendship to him and blurted out, "My brother! I can't believe I am shaking my brother's hand!"

Andy's inner joy spread to his smile, shone from his eyes, and dashed away the last remnant of doubt he had battled. No matter who he was, his sister accepted him!

"Allison, this means much to me." His voice wavered, and he cleared his throat. "More than you will ever know. Welcome to our home and family." He turned to find his wife standing back, smiling her beautiful, gracious smile of acceptance for this unknown sister and family.

"Come, Sarah," he motioned her to his side, knowing she, too, rejoiced that this meeting was what he had prayed for.

"Now I want to meet your husband and family." Andy extended his hand to his sister's husband and her two children. As the two men shook hands, Allison keenly realized what a different world she was in. This bearded, plainly clothed Amish brother and his wife contrasted with her and her family in almost every way.

Why didn't Andy tell me he was Amish? Or didn't it matter to him? She gazed at her surroundings. *Why, the house is huge! And beautiful!* She had been too nervous to notice details when they arrived. An open porch stretched across the front with a basement walkout beneath. *Nothing like our two bedroom rental,* she mused. Two barns, a fenced field running up the hill until it met thick trees, and another, smaller house partway down the lane added to the farm's charm. *Being Amish must be wonderful! It does feel like we are in a movie!* She choked back laughter at the thought.

"I brought a whole milk crate of pictures," she blurted out. "Would you like to see what our mother looked like?"

Would I? Andy tingled with anticipation. "Yes," he answered simply. "We will be glad to see your pictures. Let Sarah get our two-year-old and the other children. Remember, I told you we have ten children. They are waiting indoors to give us time to meet you, but I know they are impatient to come out. Let's sit here on the porch and look at your pictures and visit."

After they had settled on the porch, Allison handed her newfound brother a photo. "This is our mom," she said.

Andy's hand trembled as he took the photo, and for the first time in forty-three years he saw the face of the mother who had given him birth. Unasked questions tumbled over each other. He was eager for whatever information his sister could give him. But as Andy held his birth mother's picture, he knew that no feelings toward his birth family would ever take precedence over the love and thankfulness his heart held for Mom and Dad King.

"Allison, do you know who my father was?" Andy asked as he held the picture of his mother, who bore close resemblance to his sister. He thought he was prepared for the answer, but as soon as the question was asked he felt himself shutting down inside. The blacked-out words on the Juvenile Court papers were all he could think about. He had to focus on breathing. It felt like his life had come to a complete stop.

"He was one of our uncle's friends," she replied. The vise squeezing Andy loosened its grip. "He was a military man," Allison continued, unaware of what the revelation meant to her just-found brother. "He was eighteen years old, had a week's break, and came home with one of the neighbor boys.

"One of my aunts told me about the boyfriend, and I was able to make contact with his family after I found out about you. It's a sad story, but the parents told me that when their son realized he would be court-martialed for being involved with a minor, he took his own life with his military rifle.

"His family allowed me that one contact. After they gave me the information, they made it clear, 'Do not interfere in our lives again. That chapter is closed.'

"I saw a picture of your father, Andy. You look just like him. Same red hair, same Irish traits; you are definitely like your father."

The Grandmother

"I am glad for Andy that he has found a sister," Fanny admitted to her husband after they had gone over to meet his newly-found family. "I know he has struggled with knowing his background. I was fearful his sister would not accept him, but God has answered my prayer again."

"Yes, I'm glad, too, that she readily accepted him," Mark said. "Finding his birth family has been a good experience for Andy because he has been accepted and can put to rest the question of who his father was. Not every person who searches for his biological family will have the same good results. Some will not be wanted. Some will never find what they long to find, and others may wish they had not found out what they did, when they need to deal with further rejection."

Mark could not help thinking of their two other sons, sons who might want to search as Andy had. *What was in store for them if they did? How would their searches end?*

"Why do so many people label adopted children as inferior and look down on them?" Fanny wondered, interrupting her husband's thoughts. She didn't wait for an answer but continued. "Remember last year when we were in Florida?"

Mark nodded. "How can I forget? I could never figure out why a stranger would say, 'Your children are adopted, aren't they?' and then ask the probing question, 'How did they turn out?' "

"Yes, but God gave you the right words," Fanny reminded. "I'm sure the man had much to think about."

Her mind went back to the way her husband had answered the hurtful question when he had simply but kindly turned to the man and replied, "Do you have children?"

"Yes," the stranger had answered.

"May I ask you the same question? How did they turn out?" The man had gotten a strange look on his face, stammered around, and soon disappeared into the crowd of people.

"To think our son is part Irish! That is interesting to know!" Fanny chuckled as she steered her thoughts to something pleasant. "And isn't it interesting that both Andy's and Allison's names start with 'A'?"

"It's easy to see that Allison's Jenny and our Rose Anna are related." Mark said as he thought of the two girls, so different, yet resembling each other so closely. He smiled, remembering when Jenny came twirling onto the porch dressed in one of Rose Anna's outgrown dresses chanting, "Mommy, I'm Amish! I love this Amish dress!"

Fanny sighed. "Andy's sister and family are very accepting, but I am going to pray for the grandmother. Allison said she doesn't want to have anything to do with Andy or his family. But Mark, think of the shock of finding out your grandson is not dead! I hope Allison is right. I hope the grandmother just needs time before she accepts them.

I feel so sorry for her. What a hard, sad life she has had."

Marsha O'Connor was upset when Allison returned from the King farm and called her. "Grams! You won't guess what I have to tell you. My brother is Amish! An Amish couple adopted him! Isn't that the neatest thing?"

"Amish!" Marsha spat out in bitterness. "That is the last straw!" She became more upset when Allison brought her girls over later that same evening, and both Robin and Jenny were wearing Amish dresses.

"Look, Grandma! I'm Amish!" Jenny rushed into the room twirling around in the dress Rose Anna had given her.

"Where did you get those dresses? Weren't your clothes good enough for them?" Grandmother's scowl drew her wrinkles deeper into her skin, making her look old, cross, tired, and fragile.

"I like it, Grandma! Rose Anna gave it to me. You should see their farm. I wish we could live with them!" Jenny babbled on, unfazed by her great-grandmother's continued scowl.

"Humph!" was all her great-grandmother would say.

Several weeks after the Labor Day visit from Allison and Rod, Andy's daughter Esther approached her mother. "Mom, I wrote Grandmother O'Connor a letter. I have felt so bad for her ever since Allison said she refuses to see us. Read it, and see if it is all right." Esther handed over a neatly-written sheet of paper and a birthday card.

To Dearest Great-Grandmother,

I know we have never met. I don't know when your birthday is, but I like to think of this letter and card as the birth of a friendship between us.

I want to thank you for giving my dad a chance at life. Most people would have had a girl that young have an abortion. Because you gave Dad a chance at life, my family has had a chance, too.

Dad is a wonderful father, and my mother is wonderful too. We are a busy, happy family with ten of us children. I, Esther, am the third girl in our family with two sisters, Rachel and Sara Kate, older, and two sisters, Ruth Edna and Mary, younger. Next in line are Johnny and Jacob, followed by Rose Anna, Levi, and Elijah. We have a lot of fun together, but we also work hard.

If you don't want to accept this letter, just burn it or whatever, but if you would like to meet us, I am including our phone number. You will need to leave a message, as our phone is not in our house. Whichever way you decide, you will always be in our hearts.

Love, your great-granddaughter,
Esther King

After Marsha O'Connor opened and read the letter from Esther, she sat stunned, unable to comprehend how someone she had never met could write a letter expressing such love. A great-granddaughter she never knew existed and whom she refused to acknowledge had taken time to write to her—an embittered eighty-two-year-old woman. Tears rolled down her cheeks, as she felt her anger slowly dissolve. The hard shell of protection she had kept firmly in place around her heart for as long as she could remember began to crumble, and with its crumbling, a loud wail rose from her troubled breast and filled her lonely house.

When her emotional torrent subsided, she sat hunched over in exhaustion, longing for another human to be in the room with her, fearful she might never have a chance to meet the family of Jan's son, fearful her pounding, hurting heart would simply give out, and she would die alone before she could talk to anyone.

Eventually she calmed and found the energy to dial Allison's phone number.

"Allison . . . I . . . this letter . . . didn't know . . ." and Grandmother O'Connor could not talk for the tears choking her throat.

"Grams! I will be right over!" Allison dashed out of her house and ran the two blocks down the street to her grandmother's house. Panic escalated with each passing second. *What has happened? Grams never cries! Never!* Allison entered her grandmother's house to find her holding a letter in one hand and wiping tears with the other.

"Grams, what's wrong?"

"I didn't know; I didn't know," Grams kept repeating when Allison noticed the card lying on the table. Picking it up, she read, "To Dearest Great-Grandmother." Glancing down, she saw the signature.

"Grams, this is from Andy's girl! Did you know that?"

Grandmother nodded and handed her the tearstained letter. Allison was moved as she read the touching letter and sensed genuine love radiating through the written words. No wonder Grandmother was crying.

"They are a wonderful family and would love to come meet you, Grams. Being Amish only makes them nicer."

"I never thought of how they would feel. When I found out your mother was going to have a baby, I was furious at her. When she left home for a while before the baby was born, I was happy to be rid of the shame she had brought me. I refused to think about her and her unborn baby until she came home from the hospital alone. Only then did it hit me that her baby was my grandson! I became angry that I had been cheated out of raising my own grandson.

"When I was told he was never given hope to live, I assumed he had died at birth. I left the hospital angry at the unfairness of life." Grams' pent-up feelings spilled out as if she could not stop their torrent, and Allison listened in wide-eyed shock at her grandmother who normally made only short, crusty statements. *Grams never talks like this! Never!*

"To think they would let me believe Jan's baby had died!" Grams kept speaking, sharing thoughts with Allison that she had never shared with anyone else. "That was many years ago. Many years. My grandson dead, and I never saw him. Then Jan was killed. I was so angry at all the tragedies I had experienced in life that I refused to tell you and Brent that your mother was killed. It was weeks later until you found out.

"I'm a cross old woman. Maybe Jan's son won't like what

they find if they meet me."

Allison gave a short laugh and Grams looked at her queerly. "For sure, they will want to meet you! For sure!" Allison repeated. "Don't you like my expression? I love to hear them use it. I know Andy would say, 'For sure we want to meet her!' "

"Then call this number, Allison, before I change my mind," Marsha said suddenly. "Tell them I would like the whole family to come."

Andy Extends Help

2010

"Truman, the most important thing for you to do is accept what God has planned for you and believe that He cares about you." Andy laid his hand on the shoulder of the distraught adopted boy seeking his help.

"I wish it were different. Why can't my birth mother at least consent to see me? That's what hurts! If she would only let me meet her once!" Bitterness, hurt, anger, and rejection seemed to explode from the words Truman quietly but forcefully uttered.

Help me, Lord, Andy cried. *Help me show this young man that you love him even though his mother doesn't want to meet him.* Aloud he said, "Truman, I struggled too with rejection. My parents loved me, and I loved them. I grew up in a happy, caring family just like you. But even so, there was a longing to know my birth family. I understand your feelings. You long to know who you are, who you look like, and what your background is. You want to know why your mother did not want you, who your father is, and so on. I understand that.

"For a long time I didn't think I ever would know my birth family. Even when I started searching for them, for years, I had no success. Now in recent times, I have built a relationship with my half-sister and my grandmother. They accept me, and I am grateful to God for allowing their acceptance. However, I have a half-brother who wants nothing to do with me. That hurts.

"But do you know what has helped me, Truman? You might be surprised, but for many years already God has used birds to help me with these feelings of rejection and bitterness. Have you ever seen the bald eagles that live around here?"

"I might have seen them, I don't know. I never pay much attention to birds." Truman gave a brittle laugh. *Why did I come to Andy King for advice? Changing the subject to talk about birds that I have no interest in!*

"You should start watching them, Truman. Learning about the eagles has helped me understand God better. Come, let's walk back to the woods. We should be able to get a glimpse of them today."

The love and kindness radiating from Andy melted Truman's resistance, making him willing to go along and listen. His parents had said if anyone could help him, it would be Andy King. Truman was tired of fighting his misery, and he did admire this big, quiet, kindhearted man.

As Truman looked up into the tall, leafless oak tree at the exposed eagle nest through Andy's binoculars, he found his interest piqued. He had never dreamed a bird could build a nest that size. "It's been here a little longer than I have," Andy explained. "Each year they add a few more sticks. Each year it gets a little wider and deeper. They don't build it all at once. When I first saw it, it was quite small; but look at it now, a good three feet wide and deep."

Truman and Andy found seats on a nearby rock. As they sat and watched, an eagle began circling overhead. "The Bible has quite a bit to say about eagles, Truman. It says that those who wait on God, or trust Him, will be able to soar above their problems like eagles. It says that they won't become tired and worn out, but that they can keep coming back to God and renewing their strength. It also says that God is the one who marvelously provides for the eagles, giving them everything they need."

Truman was listening to what Andy was saying, but he was also watching the eagle as it soared and swooped. He had never stopped to pay attention to them before. "I'm listening, Andy," he said softly when Andy stopped. "Keep talking."

"Well, Truman," Andy said, "God has provided for you, too, don't you think? First of all, He gave you the gift of life. Then, He found a Christian home for you, complete with parents to love you and take care of you. And best of all, He has promised to help you overcome every problem that comes your way. With His help, you can rise above them, just like that eagle is soaring above the trees."

"Thanks, Andy," Truman said after a few minutes. "You've given me a lot to think about."

"Come with me to the house, Truman," Andy said. "I have a paper with several Bible verses that have helped me tremendously. I want to give the paper to you, and I encourage you to read these verses every day."

As the men entered the house, two eagles spread their majestic wings in the dazzling blue autumn sky. Sunlight struck their glossy, dark feathers as they caught the dancing wind currents. A shrill, challenging cry rent the air above. The larger eagle dropped like a bullet before swooping upward to join its mate as together they soared higher and higher into the heavens, demonstrating once again God's power and care for all of His creation.

Epilogue
God's Hand of Mercy

February 2014

February 14, 2014, found Andy, his wife, and daughter leaving the outskirts of the city for home when suddenly Andy grabbed his chest, seized with intense pain. It took Esther several seconds to realize something was not right with her dad.

"Mom! You've got to come back here! Hurry!" At Esther's cry, their driver pulled into a shopping plaza. In a flash, Esther was out the door, trading places with her mother who had been riding in the front passenger seat.

"He doesn't respond! What should we do?" Sarah's frantic question had their driver immediately calling 911 from her phone. In less than three minutes, the rescue squad arrived and had transferred unresponsive Andy into their care.

Ten minutes elapsed from the time Andy experienced his first pains until he was stabilized at the hospital. The doctor found he had eighty percent blockage in an artery and needed to have a stent put in.

"I couldn't breathe. The pain was so bad it felt like a vise was squeezing me. I tried to talk, but couldn't, and that is all I remember," Andy recalled.

"You were fortunate that this happened when and where it did," the doctor told him gravely. "If you hadn't been able to get immediate help . . ." He left the sentence hanging, then continued. "You were living with a silent killer."

Saturday night Grandmother O'Connor called Andy's hospital room, and though Andy could not see his grandmother, he could hear the tears in her voice as she repeated over and over again, "I don't want to lose you. I don't want to lose you. I just found you. I just found you."

Each day of his five-day hospital stay, Grandmother called to make sure he was doing fine.

"Thank you, Lord," Andy prayed in thanksgiving. "Thank you for having your merciful hand over me and granting more days of life.

"My family needs me. Grandmother seems to need me, and God, thank you for needing me yet on this earth. I want to serve you faithfully as long as you give me life." Andy held his hand over his heart, feeling the strong, rhythmic pumping of life-giving blood.

Then his bedside phone rang. The caller identified herself as a biological cousin. "I just hung up from talking to your grandmother," she explained. "I hadn't talked to her in months, and as soon as I called her, she said, 'Andy had a heart attack!'

" 'Andy who?' I asked as I drew a blank, and then your grandmother proceeded to tell me all about you. I never knew any of this before, but I needed to call you. I want to come see you some time and meet this grandson of Marsha's who means so much to her."

Joy flooded Andy's soul as he put down the phone, contemplating this new development. "Thank you, Lord! I don't deserve this, but I thank you for your mercy."

Forty-eight years ago I had no name, no home, no parents to care for me. A tear slid down his cheek, wetting the pillow on which he lay. "Thank you, God, for giving me loving, godly parents and a home of safety where I was wanted and taught to love the Lord Jesus."

Andy thought of his dear Sarah. "Thank you, Lord, for my faithful companion." His mind drifted to each of their ten children. Before long they would gain two more children, sons-in-law, faithful men serving God and the church. Another tear joined the first and more threatened, but Andy's next thoughts brought a smile that started from the depths of his strong beating heart. They illuminated his face and radiated upward as he closed his eyes and finished his prayer to his merciful God.

"Thank you for life. I don't know how many more years you will grant me, but Lord God, make me a blessing and use me as you see best."

About the Author

Lily Bear and her husband David live in northwestern Ohio where she has been a homemaker for forty-one years. God has blessed them with five children and fifteen grandchildren.

Born in northern Alberta to a story-telling father, Lily had an early love for books and writing. But she admits that writing is intense work. She is thankful for her husband, who supports her and prays for her. She is also grateful to God for directing her thoughts as she writes.

Lily shares, "I had the privilege of receiving a younger brother by adoption. It has also been a joy to welcome one niece and two nephews in the same way. May this book glorify Christ and Him alone."

If you wish to contact Lily, you may write to her in care of Christian Aid Ministries, P.O. Box 360, Berlin, Ohio 44610.

Christian Aid Ministries

Christian Aid Ministries was founded in 1981 as a non-profit, tax-exempt 501(c)(3) organization. Its primary purpose is to provide a trustworthy and efficient channel for Amish, Mennonite, and other conservative Anabaptist groups and individuals to minister to physical and spiritual needs around the world. This is in response to the command ". . . do good unto all men, especially unto them who are of the household of faith" (Galatians 6:10).

Each year, CAM supporters provide approximately 15 million pounds of food, clothing, medicines, seeds, Bibles, Bible story books, and other Christian literature for needy people. Most of the aid goes to orphans and Christian families. Supporters' funds also help clean up and rebuild for natural disaster victims, put up Gospel billboards in the U.S., support several church-planting efforts, operate two medical clinics, and provide resources for needy families to make their own living. CAM's main purposes for providing aid are to help and encourage God's people and bring the Gospel to a lost and dying world.

CAM has staff, warehouse, and distribution networks in Romania, Moldova, Ukraine, Haiti, Nicaragua, Liberia, and Israel. Aside from management, supervisory personnel, and bookkeeping operations, volunteers do most of the work at CAM locations. Each year, volunteers at our warehouses, field bases, DRS projects, and other locations donate over 200,000 hours of work.

CAM's ultimate purpose is to glorify God and help enlarge His kingdom. ". . . whatsoever ye do, do all to the glory of God" (1 Corinthians 10:31).

The Way to God and Peace

We live in a world contaminated by sin. Sin is anything that goes against God's holy standards. When we do not follow the guidelines that God our Creator gave us, we are guilty of sin. Sin separates us from God, the source of life.

Since the time when the first man and woman, Adam and Eve, sinned in the Garden of Eden, sin has been universal. The Bible says that we all have "sinned and come short of the glory of God" (Romans 3:23). It also says that the natural consequence for that sin is eternal death, or punishment in an eternal hell: "Then when lust hath conceived, it bringeth forth sin: and sin, when it is finished, bringeth forth death" (James 1:15).

But we do not have to suffer eternal death in hell. God provided forgiveness for our sins through the death of His only Son, Jesus Christ. Because Jesus was perfect and without sin, He could die in our place. "For God so loved the world that he gave his only begotten Son, that whosoever believeth in him should not perish, but have everlasting life" (John 3:16).

A sacrifice is something given to benefit someone else. It costs the giver greatly. Jesus was God's sacrifice. Jesus' death takes away the penalty of sin for everyone who accepts this sacrifice and truly repents of their sins. To repent of sins means to be truly sorry for and turn away from the things we have done that have violated God's standards (Acts 2:38; 3:19).

Jesus died, but He did not remain dead. After three days, God's Spirit miraculously raised Him to life again. God's Spirit does something similar in us. When we receive Jesus as our sacrifice and repent of our sins, our hearts are changed. We become spiritually alive! We develop new desires and attitudes (2 Corinthians 5:17). We begin to make choices that please God (1 John 3:9). If we do fail and commit sins, we can ask God for forgiveness. "If we confess our sins, he is faithful and just to forgive us our sins, and to cleanse us from all unrighteousness" (1 John 1:9).

Once our hearts have been changed, we want to continue growing spiritually. We will be happy to let Jesus be the Master of our lives and will want to become more like Him. To do this, we must meditate on God's Word and commune with God in prayer. We will testify to others of this change by being baptized and sharing the good news of God's victory over sin and death. Fellowship with a faithful group of believers will strengthen our walk with God (1 John 1:7).